INHERITED TOUCH

Judith A Green

First published by Busybird Publishing 2020
Copyright © 2020 Judith Green

Print: 978-1-925949-89-6
Ebook: 978-1-925949-98-8

This work is copyright. Apart from any use permitted under the Copyright Act 1968, no part of this publication may be reproduced, stored in a retrieval system or transmitted in any form or by any means, electronic, mechanical, photocopying, recording or otherwise, without the prior written permission of Judith Green.

Cover Image: Unknown
Cover design: Busybird Publishing
Layout and typesetting: Busybird Publishing

Busybird Publishing
2/118 Para Road
Montmorency, Victoria
Australia 3094

I acknowledge the Traditional Owners of Country, past, present and future.

For Mum who trusted me to tell the stories.

For Dad who respected the women of the stories.

The women of Inherited Touch *are my ancestors.*

Their stories passed through generations and several story tellers before I heard them. I have written their stories as I recall they were told to me.

My personal stories are written as I experienced them or as hindsight clarified my perceptions.

There may be those who have heard my ancestors' stories differently or disagree with elements of my personal stories.

But these are my memories, my experiences, told from my perspective.

Contents

1. Peeling the Onion ... 1
2. Seasons ... 5
3. Around the kitchen table ... 11
4. Mary Yvonne Jefferies (Avery) ... 16

LETTERS TO MY GRANDMAS AND AUNTIE ... 25
5. Frances Alice (Allie) Smart (Jefferies) ... 27
6. Mary Amelia Jefferies ... 32
7. Alice Edith Hancock (Avery) ... 40

MY GREAT GRANDMAS ... 49
8. Alice Clark (Smart) ... 51
9. Catherine (Kate) Creswick (Jefferies) ... 58
10. Amy Boon (Hancock) ... 65
11. Charlotte Chamberlain (Avery) ... 70

MY GREAT GREAT GRANDMAS ... 79
12. Phoebe Hall (Clarke) ... 81
13. Jane Woodall (Smart) ... 87
14. Mary Hughes (Creswick) ... 98
15. Eliza Hunt (Jefferies) ... 104
16. Ann Toop (Boon) ... 110
17. Lavinia Bishop (Hancock) ... 116
18. Harriet Roberts (Chamberlain) ... 123
19. Martha Shackley (Avery) ... 128

MY GREAT, GREAT, GREAT GRANDMAS ... 135
20. Mary Murphy (Hall) ... 139
21. Sarah Bowtell (Clark) ... 146
22. Mary Ann Kay (Kain) ... 151
23. Charlotte Foote (Smart) ... 156
24. Eliza/Elizabeth Bickford (Boon) ... 160
25. Tamson/Thomazine/Thomasina Bray (Bishop/Boundy) ... 162

MY GREAT, GREAT, GREAT, GREAT GRANDMA ... 167
26. Ann Whiteway (Bickford) ... 171
27. Neatening the Threads ... 175

Yvonne as a young woman

1
Peeling the Onion

The air was freezer cold as I scurried up the slight incline from the car park to Yarriambiack Lodge, the aged care facility where Mum now lived. Stepping through the automatic doors I was swaddled in intense warmth similar to that of a Grandma hug.

Mum's smile was never limited to the shape of her lips. Their movement as they curved upwards triggered the light in her eyes setting her vocal cords in motion, 'Hello Dear'. The greeting rarely changed from my primary school days when however much I loved school I looked forward to going home, continuing through secondary school with teenage dramas, peer pressure, real or assumed, subject choices and career paths to be explored, the sameness of the greeting a security blanket as the world around me was changing. When I left home at the end of secondary school to attend Melbourne Kindergarten Teachers College a strong, lingering hug was added.

The laughter lines around my eyes were a little more pronounced than I wanted them to be, a small child called me Ma, his abbreviation of Grandma, two sons delighted in calling me the 'old grey fuzz ball' and my husband and I were discussing retirement, no longer in the distant future, when I sensed Mum's hug was a learnt formality rather than an embrace, her smile often limited to the shape of her lips.

Dementia, I've been told, is like peeling an onion. Layer upon layer upon layer of living discarded until little, if anything remains. The forgetfulness disturbing, the repetition of stories frustrating, but the warping of Mum's personality from loving and caring to nasty and vindictive was one of dementia's cruellest barbs. We had what I called 'Mum days' and 'dementia days'. As 'dementia days' huddled closer together, Dad reached a decision which came close to destroying him. He could no longer care for the woman he loved. My brother and I supported him in the decision he made.

My steps slowed as I turned towards Heath Street (the then four wings of Yarriambiack Lodge named after native flora). It was as familiar as walking into my own home. My eyes lingered on a mural along one wall depicting a yesteryear rural scene. Parrot decals flew across another wall. A giant clock hung above the mantel piece, its numerals kind to eyes dimming with age. Armchairs hugged the space surrounding the fireplace where a pretend log fire burnt brightly. Mum was seated in one of the armchairs. Is today a 'Mum day' or a 'dementia day'? I yearned to experience one of the now rare 'Mum days'.

'Hello Mum.'

'Where's your father?' her words stinging.

'He'll be up later,' I replied, attempting to master a non-confrontational tone. However much I understood what dementia was doing, the pain of what Mum was becoming was not diminishing. 'It is still morning, nearly your lunch time.'

I pulled a chair close to Mum.

'He usually comes later.' Her words softened. 'He stays and has tea with me.' She gazed towards the end of the large room, eyes unblinking. What memory thread was she trying to connect? A sigh whispered. She turned to me.

We talked about the weather; how cold it was that day. She worried about having a warm coat in case she needed to go outside. She thinks someone has taken her warm coat. I assured her it was still hanging in her wardrobe in her room.

'Are you sure?' she queried.

'Yes, I'm sure.' I replied. The conversation was a familiar one. If not a coat, a blouse or slacks or shoes were missing or stolen. I sometimes joked with those who understood, there was a fourth dimension in Mum's room where items disappeared for a time, then miraculously reappeared. Mum was pleased those who 'stole' the items eventually returned them. Sometimes I would find a comb or a letter or a slipper in an unexpected place. Rather than show pleasure Mum wondered why I put them there so she couldn't find them. Although frustrating I developed a rather warped sense of humour. It was preferable to crying. Dementia *is* like peeling an onion. As layers of living are discarded tears flow frequently as the pungent odour of the onion is released.

It was a brief visit to Warracknabeal this time.

'I'm going back to my house today,' I told Mum, choosing my words carefully. I'd learnt to say 'house' not 'home'. 'Home' evoked a venom filled response, 'It's okay for you, you can go home whenever you like. You took me from my home and stuck me in here.' Words left no visible scar. However right, however necessary for Mum's well-being our decision had been, her poisoned words kept the wounds open, even though I knew they were dementia words not Mum words.

Mum was silent.

'I'm going back to my house today,' I repeated, wondering if she hadn't heard me.

Suddenly, she grabbed both my hands with her weakened, gnarled arthritic hands. I was surprised at the strength in her prolonged grasp.

'Don't go,' she implored me. Her faded, watery-blue eyes begging as her words were begging. 'I wish you didn't have to go.'

I hesitated, again choosing my words carefully.

'I have to go back to my house. I have to go back to Michael.'

Mum released my hands so suddenly they collapsed onto the arm of her chair.

'I know,' she whimpered, 'I know you do.'

I was fully aware of my physical surroundings. The soft footsteps of a staff member setting the tables for lunch, bright red-checked tablecloths, small vases of flowers in the centre of each table for four, cutlery for a main course and sweets, a side plate and a glass. The smell of cooked meat and vegetables soon to be served on dinner plates and placed before each resident seated in their familiar position in the dining area. It wasn't home but was as close to home as such a facility can be.

My physical surroundings receded into the background. I was drawn into another time and place, drawn into Mum's peeled-away-dementia-world when she was a young child saying yet another goodbye to her dying Mum. Except this day Mum is playing the part of her Mum. I'm cast as Mum as a child.

*

Mum was four days short of her tenth birthday when her mother died. She lived with her paternal grandparents and a maiden Aunt in Warracknabeal, separated from her parents in Broadford by two long train journeys. Mum's mother was cared for by her mother in the eight years it took TB to claim her life. Mum visited her parents on a regular basis. There were many goodbyes similar to the one Mum was exposing me to for the first time today.

A jagged ball of pain rode my breathing. The pain of a dying mother separated from her only child, the pain of a little girl watching her mother die, the pain of Mum's grandmother caring for her dying daughter aware of her granddaughter's struggle watching her mother slowly die as she herself had watched her own mother die of TB when she was just ten years old, the pain of goodbye for each of them at the end of Mum's many visits, the pain of Mum reliving those many goodbyes as I farewelled her at the end of my many visits, my own pain watching Mum succumb to dementia's greed.

As the weight of generations of grief threatened to suffocate me, I relived the strength of Mum's old hands grasping mine as her mother's frail hands once grasped her hands – relived the strength in generations of inherited touch.

2
Seasons

I knew the seasons not by the calendar hanging on the wall but by life cycles on display within the paddocks.

    green tinges static marching along man-made furrows
        lush growth nurturing developing heads of grain
     baled hay edging paddocks
        golden stalks heavy with grain awaiting the harvester's blades
    stubble paddocks – spent stalks blanketing the earth
        fallow land in readiness for seeds to be sown
    green tinges static marching

I knew the pungent odour of dust, felt the grit between my teeth in the north wind's sting, the sweet, sweet smell of rain on dry earth and the earthy perfume of winter as gumboots squelched through mud. I clutched the car door handle in winter as Dad negotiated the precarious clay corner on the three miles of dirt road to the bitumen, gazed out the back window of the car in summer watching clouds of powdered earth chasing us. I felt the crick in my neck tilting my head, just as my Dad did, in autumn searching for the first rains, in spring searching for rains to nourish growing crops for a good harvest and the fruitless, despairing search for clouds during a drought.

Beyond the yearly seasons I experienced the long-term weather cycle, checked Lennox Walker's long-range forecast as my parents did. Witnessed years when heavier-than-usual rain filled the crab holes, creating yellowed patches in the crops because the ground was too sodden. Years when crops were undernourished, stunted and golden stalks were not weary from carrying heavy heads of grain. Years when rain fall was great, but at the wrong time, years when total rain fall was poor but at the right time.

*

Despite the uncertainty of farming, despite the reliance on nature's elements none of us can control, my growing up was safe, secure and joyous. Mum and Dad loved one other, they loved my brother and me. I had grandparents and Auntie. They were old, of course. The perspective of old changes as we mature but as a child there is a wonderful sense of security in the ancient age of grandparents. They have been around forever, when horses pulled the plough through paddocks, dragging wagons loaded with bags of wheat to the railway station. They remembered Federation, WWI, the depression and WWII. Mum and Dad could only remember the depression and WWII. My grandparents talked about their parents who were born in Australia a very long time ago (or so I thought), about their grandparents some of whom came to Australia on sailing boats. Auntie lived in the little cottage her Dad built when he was married. Each time I sat in the old rocking chair in the kitchen near the fire it felt like the rickety house was held together with stories and memories, but I didn't think it was rickety then, just old with an outdoor bathroom and a toilet down the back.

I was nearly four when Mum gave birth to my brother. Accepted practices in maternity wards in the 1950s were mothers were in hospital for two weeks and children were not allowed to visit. One sunny afternoon Dad took me up the hospital. We stood outside on the soft, squishy lawn, obviously heavily watered as my brother was born in March, the end of summer when most lawns were dry and crisp. Dad lifted me up onto his shoulders as Mum wheeled the bassinet up to the windows. She then lifted my brother out holding him up so I could see him. It was disappointing really. Everyone said I'd have a little brother or sister to play with. No one told me how small babies are (even healthy full-term babies) or how long they take to grow to be able to play with them. Dad still had all his farm work to do so Auntie and my Grandma (Dad's Mum) looked after me. I think there may have been a little competition between the two of them as to who 'looked after me the most'. Consequently 'missing Mum' isn't something I associate too much with the birth of my brother.

However, I did associate missing Mum and Dad with having my tonsils out when I was four years old. Parents were permitted to visit only during designated visiting hours. I cried when Mum came because I wanted to go home and kept crying because I knew she wouldn't take me with her when she left. The new book Mum had brought me was of no comfort as she walked from the room without a backward glance. Didn't she know how long I cried and cried staring at the door just in case she changed her mind and came back? Mum's best friend, Laurel, who was also my Dad's cousin, was in the maternity ward which was close to the children's ward. She could hear me crying and wanted to come and comfort me. Children weren't allowed into the maternity ward, neither were mothers allowed out! The doctor let me go home early. He was afraid I might start to bleed I was so upset.

My brother and I were part of a family unit. There were times when the world revolved around our needs but there were times when the needs of others took priority. When our grandparents or Auntie were unwell, they would come and stay with us. Dad had one brother, so he and his wife shared the care of Dad's parents. Auntie was a single lady often living with us for extended periods of time. She was warm, generous and somewhat lenient with my brother and me in regards to discipline. Mum often shopped with Auntie and Auntie often bought me an ice cream. Apparently, one day I asked for an ice cream as soon as we got to the shops. Auntie instantly said 'Yes'. Mum instantly replied, 'NO!' believing I was coming to expect this every time rather than as a treat. I reacted in the only way a three-year-old could to get my own way and started screaming my objections. Mum and Auntie completed their shopping with me still stating my objections even more strongly on the way home as no ice cream eventuated despite my demands. I don't recall this incident but was reminded of it at appropriately embarrassing times in my adulthood. In fact, I don't remember ever throwing a tantrum. Mum said, 'You learnt your lesson the first time.'

During a mouse plague, in my early teens, I conveniently 'forgot' about emptying the mouse traps before letting my cat in, in the morning. The mouse trap closest to my bedroom was six or eight-sided, each side with a head hole for unsuspecting mice. These were all fully occupied on the morning in question.

Keen to get back to my book I failed to check on the path my cat took before joining me on my bed. When Dad arose later a loud knock on my door interrupted the flow of my reading. I was told to 'GET UP'. I think I responded with an unwise 'I'll be there soon' or 'I'll be there when I finish this chapter'. There was a louder knock and 'GET UP NOW'. I did. The cat had taste-tested each creature on her way to my bed, leaving the innards of the recently departed mice oozing onto the floor. My cat remained on my bed as I cleaned up her mess. I didn't make that mistake again either!

I may have learnt from my mistakes, but Mum and Dad were quick to act if life experiences became too hard. When I complained three of the senior High School girls on the school bus were bullying me (I was nine years old), Mum and Dad visited the Headmaster to make a complaint and spoke to the bus driver. It was a relief for us all when the three girls finished school. I wasn't the only one being bullied.

Likewise, when one of the primary school teachers kept me in after school making me miss the bus home (when he knew I was a country student), then dismissing me into the playground with no adult around for support, Dad visited the Headmaster. I think the conversation may have been rather heated. An eight-year-old girl left alone in an empty playground at the end of the day tends to make parents rather irate.

*

The years gathered speed. I finished High School leaving home to study at Melbourne Kindergarten Teachers College in Kew. It was a long way from home but weekly letters from me living at the Kew Baptist Youth Hostel to the family on the farm and the return letters set a pattern for the weeks. I looked for Mum's familiar writing on the envelope savouring the news inside. How sweet the ordinary is when one is a long way from home.

I finished Teacher's College spending my first year at Boort Pre-School. The next year Michael and I married. I moved back to Melbourne to teach and live. We bought a house and in time, after a few medical hiccups, we had our two sons. Still the letters flowed between phone calls and visits – the four of us to the farm or Mum and Dad to us.

Occasionally I'd feel a tad uncomfortable about remarks my brother made, particularly about Mum and the way we were brought up. While the discomfort never truly went away neither did I dwell on it. I could see no reason to distrust my brother. The danger of such a trust is that I failed to notice not only the increasing number of fractures but the severity of their depth.

Our boys grew, started school, finished school, Mum and Dad had some often-talked-about holidays within Australia. Still the letters flowed as did the phone calls and visits. There came a time when Mum seemed to be aging faster than Dad with Dad commenting on occasional 'bad' days he had with Mum. I would visit. All seemed well. I believed Dad but hadn't witnessed the 'bad' days for myself. Gradually the bad days became more frequent. Mum had difficulty hiding such days or nights when I was visiting. My visits became more frequent. At the same time I walked away from kindergarten teaching, a job I loved, over an ethical matter. Telling the truth was flung in my face. I was not asked to lie but I was admonished for reporting inappropriate actions of a staff member to the appropriate authorities and informing a child's parents of behaviour which was of concern to me. 'Why do you have to report these things?' I was asked. 'If nobody knows it doesn't matter.' My workplace was no longer a safe place for me, nor did it reflect the values I lived by.

As Mum's dementia worsened, she accused my brother and his wife of bullying her and manipulating Dad, accusing Dad of not being the man he used to be. The challenge with dealing with people with dementia is sorting truth from fabrications, but I was also becoming increasingly uncomfortable with what I was witnessing myself. Whenever I asked questions of the brother I had previously trusted and his wife, their answers were delivered with the sharpness of a surgeon's scalpel plunged deep into the flesh of our family unit, gradually severing and discarding me and my questions as one would a cancerous growth.

There came a day, a terrible day indelibly imprinted on my mind, when I witnessed the full force of my brother's verbal abuse of Mum and control over Dad. I saw my decent, respectful, honourable Dad cringing backwards, making no attempt to stop my brother's thunderous verbal tirade while towering over Mum as she lay defenceless in her bed.

3
Around the kitchen table

I felt the final cut of the scalpel the day I took Dad to visit my brother and his wife for a couple of weeks, or that was what I had been told. The previous day Dad unexpectedly said, 'I don't want to live at your house or your brother's house. I want to visit sometimes, but I want to live in Warracknabeal. When I can't look after myself anymore, I want to go up to where your mother was.' I had reassured him this was okay.

On arrival at my brother's place, however, it was apparent Dad was now living there by the number of his personal belongings already in the house. I brought his case and other items from the car by myself. Dad stood between my brother and his wife, watching me. He made no move to say goodbye. I went to Dad to give him my usual kiss and hug. He kept his arms by his side. I gave him a kiss and a hug. His arms did not move. I'm not sure how long he watched me, as I walked through the room opening and closing the door to the outdoor space, down the path to the car, then driving away.

Maybe he didn't watch me at all. He used to watch me when I left his house in Warracknabeal until I turned the corner when he couldn't see me anymore. After each of my many visits I felt a great sadness looking back seeing him standing there all alone, watching me drive away, so I would keep my eyes on the road ahead but put my arm out the window and wave. On one occasion when I did glance back, I saw his arm waving in response. It dropped to his side just as the house on the corner blocked my view. I didn't put my hand out the window and wave on that final day. I pulled over several kilometres down the road when I found a safe place to park. I sat there until my vision cleared.

*

In the months following Mum's death the images of her final days were the only images I could recall. It was as if in her dying I'd lost who my Mum was. Now I'd lost my Dad before his death.

*

Many months later I returned to Warracknabeal to visit people I trusted. It was always good to visit Auntie Laurel. Both of us enjoyed a really good chat and neither of us drank tea or coffee.

I wasn't sure what Auntie Laurel had been told about me, but her welcome was as warm as it always was. We talked about my family and her family, what was happening around the town or on the farms. Amidst the steady flow of conversation, she casually mentioned how much she appreciated Dad's visits, how he regularly came up from my brother's place. He looked well but she worried about him driving home. It was about an hour twenty minutes one way. I agreed with her. In her kind, non-intrusive manner she had assured me Dad was okay.

The conversation took another path as Auntie Laurel recalled a holiday she'd shared with Mum, part of which was to visit Mum's Uncle Ferg and Auntie Mavis in Orange. The story was a familiar one but as Auntie Laurel talked I almost heard Mum walk in the back door, into the kitchen and sit on the spare chair at the kitchen table. She was much younger then, before Dad was part of her life, her hair still black, her eyes still a vivid blue.

Uncle Ferg was a Bank Manager. It held a certain social status in the era when Mum and Auntie Laurel were young women. This probably didn't worry Uncle Ferg but Auntie Mavis took pride in such things. I really liked her, but she liked to play the lady. The hours on the bus to Orange passed quickly with Mum and Auntie Laurel active participants in the ebb and flow of talk between passengers and bus driver. A few days after arriving in Orange Auntie Mavis took Mum and Auntie Laurel shopping. As they walked along the street a loud wolf whistle rode the air waves towards them. Turning towards the source of the whistle Mum and Auntie Laurel recognised the bus driver. They waved as the bus drove past. 'Do you know that man?' a mortified Auntie Mavis demanded. These two young women known for their honesty and integrity shrugged as innocently as possible, but I think they had trouble suppressing their giggles. I'm sure Uncle Ferg roared with laughter when he heard it. That day it was worth more than a truck load of diamonds to me. The image of Mum's final days began to recede as I hugged the story of a wolf-whistling man, Mum, Auntie Laurel and a horrified Auntie Mavis to myself.

Later the same day I visited Faye and Jim. I didn't need to tell them about my brother and his wife. They had seen some of this for themselves. Faye especially had experienced Mum and Dad's kindness when Faye's husband, Mum's half-brother, had times of serious ill-health and in the final weeks of his life they'd been there to support and assist in practical ways. Faye and Jim were family and we talked of what their families were doing and people I knew in the town and so the conversation flowed. At one stage I expressed concern, 'Dad will be dead and buried before I even know he is dead.' Faye promised, 'Not if I find out first you won't.' It was a promise Faye kept when Dad did die. Michael and I were thousands of miles away in Ireland. The news of Dad's death made public too late for us to get home for the funeral. But it meant our sons, Peter and David, could attend their much-loved grandfather's funeral. It is a kindness I will never forget.

*

Amongst Mum and Dad's belongings were several calico bags containing family photos. In one of the bags are two small snapshots of Mum, taken when she was probably about eight years old and visiting her parents in Broadford. In one photo she is bottle feeding a pet lamb. In another she is bottle feeding a dog. Apparently, the dog was very jealous of the attention the lamb received and had to be bottle fed as well. It is funny to look at, but I think my pleasure was in seeing the delight on Mum's face and hearing the laughter in her voice at the silliness of bottle feeding an adult dog. Inside the house Mum's mother was slowly dying as were two of her mother's siblings.

In the background of the two photos Mum so treasured is her Grandmother. She's in her everyday working clothes – copious apron with a bib and a sun hat. Close to the chook house, I wonder if she's going to collect the eggs. The aprons of another era served many purposes, firstly they kept clothes clean but the wearer could lift the hem of the apron up to her waist creating a wonderful receptacle for eggs, ripe tomatoes, kindling for the fire or whatever needed to be carried inside when there was too much to be held in the hands. The hat Dad always wore served a similar purpose. Sometimes he'd proudly walk into the kitchen, hat upside-down in his hands, filled with mushrooms he'd found in the paddock. 'Where did you find those?' would be Mum's delighted response.

If summer was yabbying time, late autumn was mushroom picking season. When I was young, I didn't like mushrooms, but I loved the earthy smell as Mum cooked them and the fun in searching beneath the trees in the paddocks for the food treasure. Auntie especially savoured these broad flat mushrooms and she too enjoyed the search as she talked of mushroom searches of long ago. Today mushrooms are available in the shops all year round. I think we've forgotten the anticipated pleasures of foods previously only available at certain times of the year. Many of the mushrooms available in the shops today are nurtured in a pristine environment lacking the flavour of those nurtured in the raw earth beneath the trees.

The various images of Mum drifted as I settled down to sleep that night – dying Mum, giggling Mum, small girl Mum. The significance of the individual images was not only the way they merged into a picture of Mum but the way they merged into Auntie Laurel's story, into Faye and Jim's story, into my story, as did each of us into Mum's.

My sense of guilt in my inability to forgive and forget my brother and his wife for what they had done surfaced, as it often did, in those silent moments at the edge of sleep. Just as the blankets on the bed gave me warmth as I slept, the quote from psychotherapist Viet Ngyen-Gilhamm in Anne Deveson's book, *Resilience*, gave me solace: 'People have been taught to forget the past and to forgive, and the result is their feelings are frozen. Unless you can revisit the past, you can't write a new chapter.'

4
Mary Yvonne Jefferies (Avery)
3rd May 1927 – 18th October 2014

Nabulwinjbulwinj (pronounced Na-bull-win-bull-win) is a dangerous spirit who eats females after striking them with a yam. It is one of many rock art paintings we saw at Nourlangie in the Kakadu National Park. Our guide explained each painting has layers of meanings. A child is told the basic story as would non-indigenous people. As the child matures the next layer and the next and the next is revealed at the appropriate level of maturity. Maturity is not necessarily attached to a specific chronological age.

Dear Mum,

My bed was covered in piles of clothes I was trying to sort out – what would I take with me and what would I leave behind, when Dad knocked on my bedroom door. It was a few days before you and Dad drove me to Melbourne to start my three years at Melbourne Kindergarten Teachers College. 'Whenever you go out,' Dad said, stepping around the open suitcases on the floor before standing with his hands in his pockets. There was no room to sit on the bed. 'Always make sure you have enough money in your purse to catch a taxi home. Then if you don't like where you've gone or the people you've gone with you can leave. Make sure you can look after yourself.' It was the one piece of advice Dad gave me. You made one request of me. 'Write home each week so we know you are okay.'

For over forty years from the day I waved goodbye to you outside the Kew Baptist Youth Hostel to the time dementia claimed your capacity to write a letter, our sending and receiving of letters created a pattern in my week. Even as dementia cruelly erased so much you never quite lost the memory 'of all those letters we wrote'.

Through the early years of study and missing home, the joy of marriage, the arrival of children we thought we'd never have, the semi-organised chaos of growing children and all their commitments, work responsibilities, children leaving home and marrying and the arrival of grandchildren, your letters arrived every Tuesday. Every Wednesday I posted my reply. Some weeks there was little news, we'd resort to discussing the garden and other mundane matters, other weeks the letters were rich with happenings, but irrespective of the quantity or quality of the words filling the pages the letters arrived and departed as per the established routine.

It's been several years now since this constant was deleted from my life, yet the imprint is so deep I double or triple check the letterbox on a Tuesday. Each Wednesday morning, I wonder what it is I have forgotten to do.

Viewed from afar our letters were a chronology of change. Not change in the ordinariness of weekly news but change from one year to the next, one decade to another, change in family relationships, in interests and hobbies. Life experiences and age accumulated for us all. Sometimes we forget we never stop changing or maturing. Not until death claims us.

You caught me by surprise one day, a few months after you went into residential care when you said,

'This is the first time I've ever slept in a bed by myself in a room by myself.'

'Is it?' was my surprised response.

You seemed surprised at my surprise.

'You knew that,' was your sharp retort.

My mind speed-searching in the silence that followed for snippets of stories you'd given me since I was a little girl.

'When my Mum was diagnosed with TB,' you continued, 'I went to live with Grandma and Grandpa and Auntie. There were only two bedrooms. Grandma and Grandpa had one. I shared the other one with Auntie. I slept in Auntie's bed with her until I married your Dad.

I nodded. Sharing double beds with siblings or relatives was common before my time.

'Then the year I lived in Broadford with Mum and Dad in Grandma's house I had to sleep in Grandma's bed because the other rooms had people sick with TB in them.'

The snippets like pieces of a jigsaw puzzle were slotting into place.

'Then I married your father and had to share a bed and a room with him.'

'You aren't complaining about that, are you?' I dared to comment.

'No,' you smiled. You didn't elaborate. The warmth and intimacy of your relationship with Dad contained not in your initial smile but in the easy silence settling between us as your face relaxed into its before-dementia softness.

I'm sorry, Mum, for failing to connect your stories, for failing to understand the first time in your life when you fell asleep in a room and your bed by yourself, when the only sound of breathing was your own was in a time of your life when confusion stalked your every moment. I'm sorry, Mum, for failing to understand your fear of 'that place on the hill'. My decision about your care would be no different, I just wish I'd understood the reason for the depth of your fear.

You never spoke of how you felt when your Mum died, not even to Dad. Kept the emotions to yourself. In your early seventies you decided to put a small plaque on your mother's unmarked grave in the Broadford Cemetery. Despite the years since you'd visited the cemetery you knew where to park the car, which gate to enter, the location of your grandfather's grave, those of your mother's siblings and where your mother is buried – all unmarked. Three adults (you, Dad and me) gathered around a now flattened plot with a small, shiny new plaque. In solemn silence broken only by bird calls from nearby trees I saw a little girl standing where you were standing, a little girl now an old woman still grieving the loss of her Mum. An absence of tears doesn't mean the sadness ever went away. Dad held your hand tightly in his. Eventually you said, 'It's time to go.' You didn't let go of Dad's hand until we reached the car and he opened the door for you. A few kilometres down the road, after you'd had time to pack away your emotions once again, you broke the silence planning where we would have lunch.

Anne Deveson concludes her book, Resilience, with a quote from the writer V. S. Naipaul, 'Grief never leaves you, but it mutates into a deepening awareness of the greater capacity for love, and an extraordinary awareness of the interconnectedness of life.'

If I felt a heightened awareness of your lifelong grief for your Mum, I was also acutely aware of your resilience. As the stories you'd told me over the years slideshow clicked through my head I pondered on how you developed such resilience from those early years of much sorrow.

'My strongest memory of my Mum,' you said, 'was standing in the doorway of her bedroom talking to her.' I felt sad, for you and your Mum because you couldn't sit on the bed or cuddle up to her. But you remember the talking, the conversation, the interaction between the two of you. What did you talk about? What did I talk about with you? We'd sit and chat for an afternoon sometimes and if Dad asked what we'd talked about neither could remember.

'Mum did Crossword puzzles all the time,' you told me. Did you inherit a love of Crosswords from your Mum or was it learned behaviour? Either way I don't have a love of doing Crosswords. I do have your mother's dictionary and your Thesaurus side-by-side on my bookshelf though.

'Mum did embroidery,' you told me another time producing a piece your mother had made for you. 'Auntie made this into a little bag for me so I could use it.' You handed this treasure to me to keep. I too enjoy doing embroidery, although you preferred creating tapestries rather than embroidery.

'You got your love of reading from my mother and from me,' you said proudly. You'd be equally proud to know our two sons have inherited the same love of reading, as have our two grandchildren, your great grandchildren. Several books your Mum gave you sit on the same bookcase shelf at our home with your mother's dictionary, a book of poetry by Ella Wheeler Wilcox and a prayer book.

These are mementos of living, not dying. Memories of life, not death.

The stories of your first ten years of life oscillate between Broadford and Warracknabeal.

The many train trips with Auntie from Warracknabeal to Melbourne, an overnight stop with Auntie's cousins who lived near the Victoria Market. The train trip with Auntie to Broadford to stay with your Broadford Grandma and your parents. The reverse trip for Auntie who would return at the end of your visit to pick you up and you'd travel back to Warracknabeal together.

'I always wanted to be a gutter sweeper,' you laughingly informed me once. 'When I was little the boy next door and I used to watch the gutter cleaner. We decided it was what we wanted to do when we grew up.' I'm not sure what the boy next door eventually did. You became a bookkeeper.

Your father wrote twice a week to his Mum, your Grandma in Warracknabeal while he lived in Broadford. I'm impressed with twice *a week but even more impressed at a man doing so. My apologies to all men reading this but, in my experience, it is generally women who do the letter writing! It was your job to go down and collect the mail on the late afternoon train on a Friday. Your Dad's letter would be in that mail.*

One of your not-fondest memories was getting head lice when Auntie combed kerosene through your hair 'for hours and hours 'until all nits and eggs were gone.

Your first year at school was spent in Broadford where you would sometimes accompany your Grandma taking the cow down to the Common in the mornings and bringing it back at night. You walked to school by yourself in Broadford and Warracknabeal. We saw your Grandma's house on a visit to Broadford driving the route you walked to school. 'It was a long way,' you exclaimed. 'I thought it was only a long way because I was only six, but it really was a long way.' Then you added, 'Grandma couldn't take me, she had to look after the sick ones.'

This triggered another memory of walking home from primary school in Warracknabeal.

'I was walking home from school one day when Grandpa went past in his horse and wagon. He would usually just wave but this day he stopped and picked me up and took me home. He thought I wasn't well because I was walking funny.' You said you spent six weeks in hospital with heat stroke or something.

Your stories all involved people you had relationships or friendships with. When all I could focus on in those first ten years was the death of your mother coming four days before your tenth birthday. You were never alone. You may have been separated from your parents, but you were part of other people's lives as they were part of her life. There must have been sadness, as you revealed to me in role playing your mother's farewell to you, but there was a balance in your life when there was laughter and fun, the normal distaste of the kero treatment for nits was a funny story long after the event, but even in the story of going to hospital it was your Grandpa who picked you up and took you home. You were loved and cared for.

Then came the day your Mum died. You never said how you were told. But you spent three weeks at home. 'When I went back to school,' you told me, 'the teacher gave me a big hug. He didn't say anything, just gave me a big hug.' Then you added, 'He wouldn't be allowed to do that now, would he?' My reply, 'Probably not.' I told this story as part of your eulogy. Afterwards, Lois, the girl who used to sit next to you at school approached me to tell me she remembers the day you returned to school. The teacher had told them you had just lost your mother, so they were to be kind to you. They all rushed to meet you. I wonder if this lovely man had lost his own Mum at a young age. Whatever his background his empathy and hug were a great comfort to you.

There was one final trip to Broadford after your mother died. Your Uncle Jimmy, too sick with TB to work, wove scarves and bred canaries to sell. He gave you a scarf and a canary to take back to Warracknabeal. The canary has long gone but the scarf is now in my care amongst other treasures of no financial value but of significance in the story of your life.

By this stage your Dad had a car. He was returning to Warracknabeal to live and there would be no more trips to Broadford. Your Grandma still had two sons to care for until TB claimed their lives.

'How's the writing going?' you'd ask on a regular basis. You were always interested in whatever I was working on. I'd give you and Dad copies of my finished work. You were especially delighted if a poem was about any of my female ancestors, on your side of the family or Dad's, they were all family to you.

'I'm thinking of writing a book tracing back my female ancestors, telling their stories thinking about female resilience and the spirit of community connectedness, how important a sense of belonging is.'

You reached out, grabbed my hand, holding it tightly.

'You can tell the story of my Mum and Grandma,' you exclaimed. Your smile reflected in the sparkle in your eyes. I nodded.

4 . Mary Yvonne Jefferies (Avery)

'Tell me more stories of your Mum and Grandma,' I asked one time.

'I've told you all the stories,' you said. 'You know them all.'

On the inside I was screaming, 'No you haven't'. On the outside my head was nodding. 'You remember you met my Grandma once, don't you?' I didn't need to answer, you'd opened the internal memory box. It wouldn't close until the story was told. 'Before we had Allan,' (which means I was probably about three) we went down to Morwell. She lived with Jean and George, my Auntie Jean. You remember her.' I nodded. 'You met my Grandma. Just once, but you met my Grandma.' It was always a delight for you to tell me I had met her. Maybe I do remember meeting my Great Grandma or maybe I think I remember because I've heard the story so often.

The planned book started and slowed to a halt, sparked into action again then sputtered shrivelling to a lifeless pulp. You'd ask, 'How's the book going?' I always had some excuse about where it was at or wasn't at, about research that needed to be done or some other 'writer's excuse'. Through the dementia years you kept asking until there came a time when you didn't ask anymore, dementia had won. Then you were gone. If I never get the book written, I thought, Mum isn't here to know I never told the stories of her Mum and Grandma. The reason for writing the book hadn't changed but somehow it was like being stuck in quicksand. The more I tried to write the quicker I sank. The burden of the promised book pulling me under.

'How's the book going?' I can still hear your voice.

'How's the book going?

When I was having my treatment for breast cancer a friend gave me a fridge magnet. 'We all stumble, every one of us ... that's why it's a comfort to go hand in hand.' Your hands, Mum, are my physical connection with your Mum and Grandma. The stories you told me maintain the connection when the physical connection is no longer there. I could not tell the stories of your Mum and Grandma without telling your story, without telling my story. That was my stumbling block. You and I would rather be washing the cups and saucers in the kitchen than leading the choir out the front. But you are the thread connecting me with those who lived before us. Our strength is not many single threads attempting to stand alone but the way the threads weave together, support one another, into a richly layered cloth of varying shades and textures.

I've gathered the stories Mum, the stories of my female forebears born in Australia and those who migrated here. Their individual names head individual chapters. Their stories interweave through the pages across time and place, across DNA and Christian faith, across this vast land we call home and the people of our extended family. They are mere snippets of the lives these women led but I've tried to discover stories demonstrating their resilience, who was there to support them when life turned their world 'belly-up' at times and what made our Eliza tremble and tumble and appear to lack resilience. When I was teaching, I read the book, A Parent's Treasure Chest – Exploring the Path to Resilience by Constance Jenkin and Ann McGennis. In it they quote Andrew Fuller, an Australian clinical psychologist, 'Resilience is the happy knack of being able to bungy jump through the pitfalls of life. Even when hardships and adversity arise, it is as if the person has an elasticized rope around them that helps them to rebound when things get low, and to maintain their sense of who they are as a person.' Bungy jumping is not an experience one can attempt alone. The participant must trust the person who has chosen and prepared the site, the person who ties the elastic around their ankles and the person who will haul them up when the jump is complete. You and I had no desire to bungy jump but we valued those who walked beside us as we experienced life's bungy jump emotions.

Love,

Judith

LETTERS TO MY GRANDMAS AND AUNTIE

5
Frances Alice (Allie) Smart (Jefferies)
1897 – 1937

Dear Grandma Allie,

I felt as though I was riding a breeze past an open window, glancing in I caught a glimpse of you alone in bed engrossed in a book. It was middle-of-the-day sunshine bright. There was another single bed in the bedroom of your mother's house, day-time neat, positioned to minimise the risk of airborne infection when your husband, my Grandpa Bob was sleeping. The breeze had a place to go. It took me with it.

'Reading gives us someplace to go when we have to stay where we are.' The American aphorist, Mason Cooley said.

Have you ever heard of an aphorist or aphorisms? Being a cross word connoisseur, I thought it a good chance you knew the words. In your dictionary it is sandwiched between aphony and aphrodisiac. An aphorism is 'a concise statement of a principle in any science; a brief, pithy saying; an adage'. In my dictionary the word aphorism is sandwiched between aphis and aphrodisiac. The meaning given in my dictionary is, 'a terse saying embodying a general truth'.

It's taken me a long time to call you Grandma Allie. You were always Mum's Mum, which you are, but somehow you weren't real to me. Rather like a cardboard cut-out. I knew your name and life dates, but I couldn't feel your touch. Mum said, 'Tell the story of my mum and Grandma' when I told her of my idea for this book. So I tried, like a traffic controller with the STOP/GO sign at road works, I controlled your stories, their placement implying significance. The traffic controller guides motorists safely through the road works, I guided your stories safely through to the end of the chapter. The words were all there, the stories recorded, but without emotion the stories are as lifeless as the road the traffic controller guides us along.

There is no way I can comprehend your sadness, your fear, when your world went 'belly-up' with your TB diagnosis. Your mum said, 'Come home and I'll take care of you'. So you and Grandpa Bob moved to Broadford. What immense trust you had in his family leaving your eighteen-month-old child in Warracknabeal in the care of her grandparents (in their sixties) and her maiden Aunt. The right decisions were made but that doesn't mean you were content and at peace.

Your mother had already nursed her husband and one daughter to their deaths with TB. When she was ten years old her mother (Phoebe) died of TB. In the ensuring years some of her siblings were to succumb to the dreaded disease. When Phoebe was seven years old, she saw her father die of TB. When Phoebe's mother died (not of TB) aged 69, only five of the at least thirteen children she'd given birth to outlived her. Most of the adult children died of TB. I'm sure you clung to hope, but you knew the path TB would take. Faith is a very fine thread of hope and trust. As you faced the inevitable, was it faith giving you joy in each new day creating resilient memories to last your daughter to the end of her days? Was the trust in your in-laws and sister-in-law a reflection of the faith they lived through their daily lives?

Mum's stories of you, the photos she treasured were not of your dying but your living. Her sadness at your death was the shortness of your living. My sadness is not my mother's sadness for she mourned you when you were no longer part of her life. My sadness is you were never part of my life.

Do you remember the pendant you received for womanliness? I think you were about twelve when you received the pendant. What were the criteria for womanliness? The photos I've seen indicate you were not one for frills and flounces. The couple of pieces of jewellery Mum gave me belonging to you also indicate you preferred understated rather than showy. The pendant and jewellery are in my treasure box now wrapped in Mum's stories.

There's an old Irish proverb, 'We live in the shelter of one another.' I rather like this. It isn't one taking control, one being stronger another weaker, it is the give and take of relationships. It is an emotional place of belonging not because you or I are rich or famous but simply because we are who we are. Whether we are sick or happy, lonely or joyous, seeking adventure or need solace, live next door or hundreds of miles apart, we live in the shelter of one another.

As I think of Mum feeding the pet lamb and the family dog, I get a sense of what this shelter really is. Her paternal grandparents and Auntie in Warracknabeal, a place she called home and the time she spent in Broadford with you and her dad, her maternal grandma and your siblings. TB was a reality to you all. It governed the choices you made. It wasn't the life you chose but you lived in the shelter of one another. Where I often feel immense sadness for Mum's early years, immense sadness for you all, I also sense a richness to those years shaping Mum into the person she was. I sense strength in you and your mum as you faced reality of what was to come but did not create a quicksand of pity stunting Mum's development. In Resilience, Anne Deveson, she wrote, 'Feeling sad doesn't mean we are not resilient – being stuck in sadness is where there may be problems.'

When you finished school, you entered domestic service travelling with a group of friends from one place of employment to another until marriage and family changed the pattern for each of you, but you maintained contact. In Mum's calico bags is the picture of a house in Toorak – she thought it one of the places you worked. A postcard from a holiday you had, sent to your husband-to-be: Dear Bob, wish you were here, Love Allie. Your best friend Myrtle was a constant in your life, photo postcards, letters and photos between you both. She was your bridesmaid when you married. I feel Myrtle's sense of loss when you died. One of my closest friends died recently. I know my sense of loss. There were letters between you and your Mum. I have no copies of these but guess they contained similar information to the ones Mum and I exchanged. To the outsider they would generally appear very dull filled with the ordinariness of everyday life, the funny anecdotes, how the garden was growing, stories about family members, the weather — nothing of significance except to those living in the shelter of one another. There is one photo postcard from you to your mum: write soon or I'll think you've forgotten me. The joy in the security of such a relationship, a gentle nudge now and then isn't a complaint more a long-distance hug maintaining the shelter you all share?

Sometimes I think about you confined to your room and wonder how you felt when Mum was there running in and out and playing. Mum remembers the windows and doors of the house were always open. It wasn't quite the air of the Swiss Alps considered so beneficial for TB sufferers but it was the best your mum could do to keep fresh air circulating through the house. There was a hospital in Melbourne you went to from time to time. Mum couldn't remember the name. Mum always had our windows open, well not during the dust storms in summer, but she loved fresh air, the smell of rain on dust, hearing the sound of sheep in the paddocks with the truck or tractor in the background. The back gate clicking shut, the dogs barking when they saw Dad, their different bark if it wasn't Dad, footsteps on the verandah. Could you see the backyard where Mum played from your bedroom window? Hear her voice talking to your mum? Did she come rushing inside to tell you what was happening, some funny story about the chooks or taking the cow to the common, the canaries Uncle Jimmy bred or the children she played with down the street? Mum remembered standing at your door talking to you, such a strong memory. Mum and I had lots of talks about important 'stuff' and the very ordinary from when I was a little girl to the very end. I think there were times in those final months when Mum and I were you and her in her dementia mind.

5 . Frances Alice (Allie) Smart (Jefferies)

To Alice and Bob,/ With love,/ From Myrtle/ Xmas 1925 the inscription at the front of the book reads. It was the first Christmas you celebrated with Grandpa Bob as husband and wife when your world was still rich with hope and anticipation. The book is a poetry book by the American poet and journalist Ella Wheeler Wilcox, apparently a rather unconventional writer of her time as you would have known. Ella wrote the poem 'Solitude' which opens with 'Laugh, and the world laughs with you;/ Weep, and you weep alone'. Close friends know us well, their gifts reflect who we are, our interests. Myrtle was your closest friend. Her choice of a gift is a cherished hint for me you enjoyed poetry.

'Grandma Allie', I whispered to myself as your name rippled from my fingertips as I typed. The stories I was telling weren't just the stories of Mum's Mum and Grandma but my Grandma Allie and Great Grandma Alice. You weren't just Mum's; you were mine too. What triggered that sense of belonging within me? Was it the split-second glimpse of you engrossed in a book or was it your love of poetry? As I hold your poetry book in my hands, caressing the suede cover – as soft as velvet – it triggers a much stronger emotion that I expected. Time and place may separate us but the cover of the book holds your touch as it now holds mine.

Dementia is an insidious disease as is TB and any other disease that claims the body or mind little bit by little bit. But every life experience shapes us in some way, exposes us to pain or sorrow, joy or happiness depending on the type of experience, provides us with the opportunities to empathise with others walking the same path. At various stages of our lives we revisit past experiences, view them from a new perspective gained as life experiences accumulate. That's where I'm at now Grandma Allie, lifting my feet from the potentially quicksand sadness of your early death recognising the resilience of living within the shelter of one another. I always thought living in the shelter of one another applied to those still drawing breath but now I realise the shelter is infinite extending to those who have drawn their final breath, but live on not only in the stories we tell but in the many layers of the stories for those willing to scratch the surface.

Love from your granddaughter,

Judith

6
Mary Amelia Jefferies
1893 - 1988

Dear Auntie,

Your letters were pages and pages folded and squashed into an envelope so thick the glue barely held it closed on its journey from you to me. I'd smile as I picked up the bulging envelope with your familiar writing from the kitchen bench at the hostel, kept smiling as I walked to my room. Tearing the envelope open was to hear your voice and feel your touch as you leant forward, reaching out to me through the words you had written. Will my hands become gnarled and misshapen as your hands did, as Mum's did as your mum's did? I feel the first twinges of arthritic pain sometimes, study my hands. Arthritic hands are not aesthetically pleasing but I felt the strength of Mum's hands clasping mine, of your hands holding mine, seen the look of joy and happiness in Mum's face and in your face as I returned the clasp. There is an abundance of love secreted in those swollen knuckles.

You wrote letters as frequently as many of us send text messages and emails. You sent postcards or picture cards to friends or relatives in towns only miles apart when telephones were 'scarcer than hen's teeth'. Your letters were not scribbled notes they were conversations of the ordinary, the everyday, the minute by minute telling of a funny or sad or significant event. Your brothers, cousins, friends, knew what was happening in Warracknabeal through your letters. The young men you knew enlisting in WWI responded with postcards from places you would never see.

The tin trunk you kept in your room, your glory box, was nearly empty when Mum cleaned out your house when you went into care. She kept the three pieces of hand painted cloth, one of supper-cloth size, the other two smaller. Why did you never finish them? Being a dress maker, you rarely left incomplete work. Mum gave me one of the pieces, supper-cloth size bound in faded newspaper to stop the material fraying and to keep its shape until the edging was stitched in place. The newspaper yellow and fragile now, since you tacked it neatly to the cloth you hand painted so carefully with the aid of a stencil. I traced the pattern of the tacking, remembered watching you when I was a little girl, your then nimble fingers inserting the needle, pulling the thread, inserting the needle, pulling the thread as you told me the importance of always tacking before sewing. Breaking the thread with your teeth when scissors weren't handy. The newspaper may have yellowed but the material is as pristine as though you had only painted it yesterday. I attempted to read the newsprint. It was still clear but folded to bind the cloth it was difficult to read enough to know what the articles were about. Turning the cloth slowly I happened upon a date. Saturday January 26th, 1915. It was Mum who told me there was one young man you cared about very deeply who never came home.

Many women of your generation never married. The Memorial in the centre of town in front of the Post Office and the Memorial Gates of Anzac Park list the names of men these women had hoped to spend their lives with. The young men died amidst the horror of battlefields we can barely imagine. The families and young women mourned individually and as a community. In time the Memorials have become part of the landscape, part of our nation's story. Those who now walk by are aware of its historical significance but no longer feel an emotional connection as you would have done.

I didn't intend to start this letter with a sad story. I intended to tell you about the day when those two little boys you loved, our sons, had grown into gangly teenagers. They had some item they wished they had enough money for. I can't remember what it was. I replied, 'If wishes were horses then beggars would ride.' They looked at me as though I was from another planet, 'Where did that come from?' I knew where it had come from. Flashback to one afternoon I was spending with you in the two bed-roomed cottage your father built. I was wishing for something, I don't remember what, when you said, 'If wishes were horses then beggars would ride.' We both laughed.

Recently Michael was walking through the house with a pair of sandals in his hand. He put them on the table while he got himself a drink of water. 'It's bad luck to put shoes on the table.' I informed him. 'That's an Auntie saying,' he responded as he finished his glass of water.

You had numerous sayings, or idioms I think is the correct terminology and many, many superstitions. Black cats, ladders, Friday 13th, shoes on tables and many others come to mind periodically, yet you were a woman of great Christian faith. When your eyesight dimmed and hearing diminished, we would often hear you murmuring Biblical passages or sections of your Prayer Book, the words imprinted on your mind you had read them so often. Words of comfort, words of hope, words of joy, words of support, your faith was deep within whatever each day would bring. When you shared my room on the farm I saw you greet each morning and farewell each night kneeling beside your bed in prayer. Your faith was not an in-your-face faith but in every breath and every step you took.

You were the gatherer of stories, the thread connecting family, the communicator and guardian of those not only within the immediate family circle but reaching out to the extended family. You were the one triggering my interest in family history, not just names, dates and places, but stories about people. How your mum gathered you all together telling you the stories of Ireland her mother had told her and her siblings as she gathered her family to her. The stories of Ireland have dispersed but the image of family gathered together is still vivid.

Your brother Fergus, the one who had 'the gift of the gab', worked for the Bank of New South Wales. Your Irish Grandma told stories of Ireland. Your mum told the stories her mum told her. Your brother Fergus told stories of those he met as he worked in various branches of the Bank, living in boarding houses as a single man. Your particular delight was the short-sheeting of his bed. Apparently he had been out for the evening arriving home after everyone else had gone to bed. I'd start smiling at this stage. I knew what was to come. He cleaned his teeth, took off his clothes, put on his pyjamas but alas when he attempted to slide beneath the sheets he discovered the dastardly deed committed by others. I'm laughing by now as you are. The best is yet to come. Now your brother Fergus was not an aggressive man. He did not resort to loud words, accusations or violent acts. He could 'think outside the square' to solve his problems in a non-confrontational manner. We're both in full-blown laughing mode now. Quietly picking up his violin Fergus started practising his musical scales. For some reason his fellow residents came to assist him in his dilemma and remade his bed for him. I can still hear your laughter, can imagine the raucous delight of you all gathered around the fire in the kitchen of the cottage when Ferg told you the story on a visit home. The very timbers of the cottage must have been rattling in delight.

By the time I knew the cottage it was old but the cracks were filled with happiness. The bathroom was outside, the toilet, laundry and woodshed away from the house. A narrow but long block there was an attached fernery-like place and a separate building simply called 'the chalet' plus a small sleep-out added to the front. It was home. Home in the richest sense of the meaning of the word. A place I liked to visit for it was still inhabited not by ghosts but by all those who shared the home with you over those many years through the stories you told.

It must have had elastic sides there were so many people who enjoyed its embrace. You and your siblings were all born in the cottage. Two died in that cottage, buried in the local cemetery many years before your parents were buried there. Your paternal grandpa, the one whose wife spent the last fourteen years of her life in a lunatic asylum, he called it home. You never knew her but the story was part of the cottage's history. 'He wasn't the same man ever again after committing her,' you said. A decision he had to make but one he forever regretted having to make. You couldn't gather her in to the family physically, but her story was part of the family story. One of your mother's siblings was gathered in after her mum died. There were others welcomed when life left them without a home. As I said, your home must have had elastic sides.

It became Mum's home when TB sent her parent's world 'belly up'. There was no hesitation. You brought her up through all the stages of childhood, the teenage years and then she married. You were never rich financially, but the most valuable wealth is not what money can buy.

You were our Auntie, a surrogate mum to my mum, a surrogate grandma to my brother and me. But you gathered what stories you knew of mum's mum so she grew up with the stories she could tell us about her mum and grandma. You made the long train trips to take Mum to see her parents on a very regular basis. We never called you Auntie Mary you were always just 'Auntie'. You filled those surrogate roles never trying to replace those who would have filled those roles.

'A poor workman blames his tools,' you told me as I muttered about something not going right and blaming whatever it was I was using, not my lack of skills. 'A watched pot never boils,' you told me as I waited impatiently for cooking to be complete. You fussed and spoilt us, made us laugh, bought me pink musk sticks because they were my favourite well into a stage of my life when I found it rather embarrassing. I bought a packet of musk sticks one day on a trip down memory lane; their flavour isn't as strong as it used to be.

You cured Dad's bad case of gastro not long after we went out to the farm. He was so weak he could barely stand by himself. At that stage Mum didn't drive. 'Give him a sip of brandy,' you said. 'That'll settle his stomach.' Mum and Dad were teetotallers, but Mum kept a bottle of brandy for the Christmas cake. She gave Dad a sip she was so concerned about him. Dad's gastro was cured. His version of the story was his throat was so raw with constant vomiting the brandy burnt all the way down. There was no way he was bringing it up to burn all the way back!

I'm not sure the story you told me about the Melbourne Cup Day was true. I'm also not sure you were in attendance or someone else told you the story. Apparently, it rained at some stage during the day, a thundery downpour often inflicted on race goers during Melbourne's spring. The ladies in all their finery were drenched. I assume the men were too, but your story focused on the ladies as their dresses shrank. The material of the day could not take a thorough soaking.

You had no fear of death, it was a part of living. This doesn't mean you didn't mourn, for you remembered the pain of your little sister dying, the sorrow when Mum's mother died, the sorrow your brother felt in the death of his wife. You visited the cemetery every week for many years putting flowers on your parents' grave and the unmarked grave where your two siblings are buried, the first born you never knew was only a few months old, the last born only thirteen months old. Mum accompanied you when she was little. I often went with you. You talked of your siblings and your parents as though their deaths were recent. There were no tears, but the sadness remained. The sadness remained yet in the telling you remembered their living. 'Don't walk on the graves,' you instructed me as we worked near unmarked graves flattened with time, wind and rain. I obeyed your instructions single-filing my feet between the graves. I still do even in the lawn cemetery where only small headstones mark the head of the grave, where lawn mowers run across the grass oblivious to those beneath the earth. I still single-file my feet between the graves.

You shared your treasures. The shoes your little sister wore who never had time to grow into her name – Annie Beatrice Victoria – you made into two pincushions. I thought it a little macabre or rather strange at the time you gave them to me, but I took them as the gift they were. There are few reminders of such a short life. You were a dressmaker and you used the pincushions, the memories of Annie Beatrice Victoria travelled with you, you passed on not only a reminder of the sadness but a reminder of the life you lived despite the sadness.

You may have been a dressmaker by day but come evening, when your dad, or Papa as you called him, arrived home with his team of horses you would go and assist him. The wagon had to be disconnected, the harnesses removed then the horses brushed, fed and watered. You were the single daughter, the spinster sister, the maiden Aunt. When your parents died you were left the little cottage. It was the only home you knew.

Your parents celebrated their fiftieth wedding anniversary a few months before your dad died. Your mum could no longer wear her wedding and engagement ring her fingers were so gnarled with arthritis. You kept them safe after your mother's death. The only living daughter, they were yours. 'Would you like them?' you asked me once. 'They were my mothers.'

Battlefield horrors robbed you of the man you would have had children with. In my early teens I'm not sure I fully understood the magnitude of the gift, but I understood the trust you had in me to keep the rings safe. I wear them from time to time, they nestle in a hidden safe-place with Mum's engagement and eternity ring and Grandma Allie's engagement ring.

'If I'm spared,' you used to say whenever we talked of next Christmas, a birthday or Easter or some celebration in the future, 'If I'm spared, I'll be there.' It became a family tradition waiting for your response. We didn't laugh out loud, just smiled. You weren't a pessimistic person more the reality none of us know what tomorrow will bring. I always thought it was an Auntie comment. Recently the daughter of one of your cousins passed away at ninety-six. When one of her sons rang to tell me we talked awhile. He told me his mum had been saying for many, many years following a birthday or Christmas or some celebration, 'This could be my last one.' She wasn't a pessimistic person either, she lived a full and happy life despite some of the sadness she carried within. I think our Irish Grandma or Great Grandma, depending on where you sit on the family tree would be smiling somewhat at the sayings curling down the tree.

You were ninety-five when you died. You were aiming for one hundred to receive a telegram from the Queen, but your body wore out with a simple cold. You died on my dad's birthday. 'Auntie would be sad she died on Grandpa's birthday,' one of our sons stated. We all agreed with him. You would be sad to have spoilt his day.

When you were welcomed at the pearly gates you may have entered with some trepidation, the memory of the mending you were doing on one Sabbath still fresh in your mind. You thought it was Saturday, not Sunday. 'Oh no,' you exclaimed when Mum explained what day it really was. 'When I go to heaven,' your mortified voice trembling as your eyes glanced over the stitches you had made that day, 'God will make me unpick all those stitches with my nose.' I'm sure you discovered the God you loved and followed so faithfully all those many years welcomed you, as is promised in the Biblical texts you knew so well, had no memory of your Sabbath stitching.

Love,

Judith

7
Alice Edith Hancock (Avery)
1888 – 1970

Dear Grandma,

Remember the day when I was eight years old and walked around to your place by myself after school? Poor Grandpa's dodgy heart skipped a few beats that day, didn't it? I'm sure you've never forgotten it and neither have I.

It was nearly the end of my Grade 3 year. For some reason another teacher (not my teacher) decided to punish me for some supposed misdemeanour and kept me in after school. He knew I was a bus student but didn't care. Finally, he let me go. The buses were gone. The school yard was empty. Everyone had gone home. Except me. I didn't cry. I wasn't a baby anymore. I was nearly a Grade 4 girl. I was too scared to go back inside to tell the teacher he had made me miss the bus. I had two options. Go to Auntie's house but she had no car and no phone. Or go to your house. You and Grandpa had a phone and a car. I didn't run but I walked very fast. When I got to your house you and Grandpa were just closing the garage door. I think you'd been shopping. I can't remember what I said but you hurried inside while Grandpa held my hand and we walked in together. I wasn't scared any more. By the time we got inside you were putting the kettle on, then Mum and Dad arrived. We sat around your kitchen table having cups of tea and biscuits. Well, I didn't have tea but I ate the biscuits. About five decades later Mum reminded me of the day I missed the bus. Funny how all those years later my hands felt as clammy as they did that day and the sound of my lunch box banging in my bag as I scurried to your place sounded suspiciously like the pounding of my heart as I relived the experience.

It is a challenge writing your stories. You were forty when Dad was born, sixty-four when I was born. You were my Grandma, and Grandma's, from a child's perspective are old. You were a reserved, quiet woman and people often equate this with being meek and mild. We both know this is not necessarily so, don't we? They obviously hadn't watched Laurel and Hardy or Charlie Chaplin with you either when your laughter echoed around the room!

Your house was always neat and tidy. In the sideboard in the lounge were some books. One of them was the Coles Book Arcade. I loved that book, never failing to be delighted by the words and pictures. One year (was it a birthday or Christmas gift?) you gave me my own copy of the book. The binding is not as firm as when I received it, but it still sits on my bookshelves. In reality some of the contents are sexist and racist but this reflects the era when the book was published. I keep it not for its contents but the memories holding the pages in place. Like the smell of Metho, it reminds me of visiting your house where small children were as welcome as adults.

On summer nights we'd sit out on your front lawn, my brother and me on the prickly lawn and adults on the chairs. Your house was over the road from the creek. As the summer sun feasted on the water the flow became sluggish, ideal mosquito breeding conditions. You'd sit with the Metho bottle in your hand ready to dab our mozzie bites with the Metho cork to stop our itching. It worked every time.

I was twelve when you and Grandpa celebrated your fiftieth wedding anniversary. Too young to understand it would have been another reminder of your two brothers killed in WWI. They were your brothers but friends of Grandpa too and were his attendants at your wedding. Two brothers and a cousin who grew up in your home were all killed in WWI. You never talked about them. A couple of years ago I visited Menin Gate and the Arras Memorial where the names of the three men are recorded, their bodies were never recovered. I left a poppy for each of them. I wasn't prepared for the immense sadness I felt for three men I had never met.

The Thirties Depression was a major experience in your life as it was for anyone who lived through it. You and Grandpa had moved to Warracknabeal around 1920 to a farm, with a mortgage, on the Henty Highway. The following is Dad's story as he told it to me. You were a woman of faith. I doubt you contemplated delivering a sermon in the Methodist Church you attended but you lived the Christian ethos of being a good neighbour. Dad told me the following story:

'When I was going to school at Batchica there'd be at least two or three horse and wagons a week, go past loaded up with everything. They just walked off their farms in the Mallee. A lot of them were Soldier Settlement blocks.

'One family stopped at the farm, the man nearly crying, his wife was sick, asking for help. Dad, (Hubert Avery) let him camp on the farm for about two weeks. Dad rang Dr Donald who told Dad to put her in the car and bring her in to him. He put her into hospital for about two weeks and told Dad to go down to Parsons (Grocers) and get a box of groceries for the family. The Dr paid for the groceries. Dad fed the horses and Mum and Dad gave them butter, eggs and milk for the family. After the wife came out of hospital they moved on. Dad got a letter from them to say they made it to Ballarat where they were able to sell their horses and wagon and find a home to live in. They thanked Dad for what he had done.

'Swagmen, often two or three a day, would call in at the house. Mum always gave them something, even if it was only some bread and butter. Once a woman knocked on the door with a ten-year-old girl. I was just a boy at the time. She was avoiding the towns because if they saw her they would have arrested her for being a vagabond. (It wasn't right. Men were not arrested but women were, especially if they had a child. It wasn't right. She was doing the best she could.) She was heading for Mildura for fruit picking. Most of them were heading up there.'

Grandpa had grown up on a farm in Antwerp close to the Ebenezer Mission and you lived on the farm for the first few years of your married life. Grandpa was friends with 'the Darkies'. The terminology is not appropriate today, but this is your story. Grandpa's friends would come looking for work during the Depression. Dad recalled one Aboriginal man 'a rough looking bloke' who his father employed. At midday you all gathered at the meal table while the Aboriginal man sat outside under a tree. He knew his place wasn't at the meal table with white people. Your response, 'I'm not running outside after him all the time,' you told your husband, 'he can come inside and sit at the table like everyone else.' To my dad's delight the man came inside and sat with you all. He also remembered the man's name.

One story I always remember with pride is your dream to go to Melbourne to study music. You were the eldest of eight and your dad could not afford to financially support this dream. An unfulfilled dream was regret you would always feel but I admire your courage to dream beyond the expectations of a woman of your era and to speak of your dream. It may surprise you, when your two sons cleaned out your home, Dad (who did not inherit your love of music) kept some of your music continuing to remind us of your talent and your dream. Some of that music is now in my safe keeping.

The dream may not have been fulfilled but you shared your music as a Church organist, at community functions and accompanying singers at social functions.

When Mum was in care, we spent a pleasant afternoon outside in the sunshine with another of the residents and some of her family. She recalled a holiday in Portland when you and Dad were staying in the same Guesthouse as her family. 'I got into terrible trouble with your mum,' this elderly lady told Dad. 'So you should have,' he retorted. 'You cried,' the lady laughed. 'It hurt,' Dad retorted. 'I was only six.' Apparently, Dad was reclining in a fold-up deck chair when this respected lady, then a teasing eight-year-old, snuck up behind him flipping the chair closed catching Dad's fingers between the wooden bars. We all laughed. 'Your Mum really ticked me off,' the now elderly lady emphasised. 'I got into really big trouble with your mum.' You were always my gentle Grandma but, on that day, you were a mum with a sobbing child. Other than some bruising no harm was done. It was just a silly childhood prank. The two main characters in the story, however, had not forgotten.

Another holiday in Portland was vivid in Dad's memory. Grandpa would stay on the farm with your first born who was twelve years older than Dad while you took Dad for a holiday during January school holidays. Dad was about eleven. Your mum wanted to go to Portland too. You didn't think she was well enough but according to Dad, 'What Grandma wanted Grandma got!' One night Dad woke up as his Grandma was trying to pull his blankets off his bed. She had either fallen getting out of bed or had collapsed. You heard their voices and came running. 'I think Mum had a bad time of it when that happened,' he told me. You had to wake the owner of the guest house initially to get a doctor. Your mum passed away later that night at the Guesthouse. You then had to wake the owner again after your mum's death to ring Grandpa to tell him what had happened. Normally Grandpa came to pick you up from Portland but this time your brother and one of your sisters came to deal with the paperwork formalities that come with death. But that wasn't the end of it. The stretcher to carry the body from the room wouldn't fit and they had to take down a wall to remove the body. I guess a small boy would find that fascinating but for you, dealing with your mother's death and a grumpy, inconsiderate guesthouse owner on your own it was a tough time. But deal with it you did.

You dealt with taking Dad down to Gippsland to visit your foster daughter. Train to Melbourne, changing trains at Spencer Street then

7. Alice Edith Hancock (Avery)

met by Doris' husband who took you and Dad by horse and cart to their isolated dairy farm. There was a river you had to go through, Dad said. He was quite impressed by the ride in the horse and cart. Dad liked Doris, keeping in touch with her until her death. I remember going to their house. Dad remembered the time you and Grandpa went to Berry Street in Melbourne to select your foster child and came home with Doris. She was older than Dad, but he enjoyed having her live in your home.

You never learnt to drive a car, Grandma, but apparently you had no problem hitching up the horse and gig without Grandpa's help to get you where you needed to go. You aren't exactly fitting the picture of a dependent woman, are you? I often think we learn more than we are taught. What we are taught are skills or information adults believe we need to know. What we learn is what we observe or experience. It becomes part of who we are without the individual realising what they have learnt. Dad respected women, not because women were good at domestic chores but because of the skills they had beyond the home front. He wasn't afraid of independent women. I often think he learnt much from you and Grandpa enabling him and Mum to create an equal partnership. Your mum was known as being strong-willed and feisty; Grandpa's Mum as formidable. We inherit far more than what our forebears may leave us in their final will and testament.

This is the first letter I've ever written to you. I never had any reason to write before as you lived close enough to visit, just ten or fifteen minutes in the car from our farm to your house. I would have written to you when I moved to Melbourne to study, but you had a stroke the day I left home and died within a couple of weeks. As I was venturing onto a new stage of my life you were slipping to the vast unknown beyond death. I didn't get to say goodbye when the rest of the family did on the day of the funeral. 'Don't come home,' Mum and Dad said, 'you've just started where you are. We've decided it would be best for you not to come home.' I wanted to come home to be with everyone else, to be there as we remembered who you were, celebrate your living. But I was overwhelmed in the newness of my new abode, in the newness of Teacher's college and the long train trip home. I didn't object but felt your loss in my loneliness as I knew no one and had no one to confide in. I grieved alone. Years later Mum confessed she regretted the decision to tell me not to come home. I too regretted not making the decision to come.

Feminist and feminism were not particularly common words in 1970 when you died. 'Women's libber' was the terminology of the time. Being traditional and conservative you were hardly a candidate for the bra-burning women's liberation movement. But the women's liberation movement didn't suddenly happen. Through generations there were rumblings and murmurings as each generation of women pushed at the boundaries, some in a quiet manner others more forthright. In your own way you pushed the boundaries, asserting your independence.

When your dad died you were left money. Being a farmer's wife, you used some of the money to buy land close to the farm your husband had. The land remained in your name. It was a family farm but the land you bought was your land. You donated money towards the building of a new hall at the Warracknabeal Methodist Church you attended. It was a donation in your name.

When I was growing up the idea of a 'glory box' was becoming obsolete. In the past a young girl would collect items for her glory box in preparation for her married life long before she was actually getting married. You gave me a couple of cup, saucer and plate sets in my early teens. But, the cup, saucer and plate sets weren't just items considered appropriate for a glory box but the essence of such items was their use in maintaining social interaction between family and friends – the cuppa with neighbours around the kitchen table, the cuppa with family who call in, the afternoon tea on more formal occasions. The cup, saucer and plate sets are a constant reminder to maintain a sense of connectedness as you did with family – the trips to visit your foster daughter in Gippsland, the day trips to Donald and St Arnaud to visit extended family, the Sunday dinners at your Mum's place after Church, the give and take of relationships, of sharing good news and bad, of being there when times are tough, or creating a safe place eight-year-old girls can run to when a teacher leaves her all alone.

I may not have embraced the 'glory box' tradition but I did follow one tradition on my wedding day – wearing something old, something new, *something borrowed and something blue. The something old was your ring with your initials AEH engraved on it, possibly a 21st birthday present. It is still in my possession and I still wear it from time to time.*

My hair is rapidly turning grey. 'Not grey Ma' our granddaughter says, 'you've got silver hair.' I rather like that idea, silver-grey hair like you had. It isn't a sign of old age, more a reminder of you. My one regret? I never heard you play the piano.

Love,

Judith

PS. Dad always remembered his third birthday. The cake you made him and the sixpenny bag of jellybeans. He always bought our sons jellybeans. 'Can I have one?' he'd ask. They would hand him one. 'I meant one for each hand,' he'd say as he held out his empty hand. They would give him one for his empty hand. Dad had a good sense of humour, as you know. Perhaps his love of jellybeans was a reminder of the happiness of his growing up.

MY GREAT GRANDMAS

8
Alice Clark (Smart)
1877 – 1964

Dear Mum,

Despite the promise 'to obey' being an accepted part of the marriage vows when you and Dad married in 1951, you refused to make that promise. Love, honour and cherish, in sickness and in health, for better or worse, for richer or poorer, you willingly promised. One of the few words of advice you gave me when Michael and I were planning our wedding was 'don't promise to obey, you don't have to do what your husband says just because he said so.' This didn't mean you didn't listen to Dad, didn't discuss matters with Dad, but it wasn't a matter of obeying for either of you. It was a matter of discussing and deciding together. When Dad made the decision he could no longer care for you he knew it was the right decision for your wellbeing, but he was torn, for he felt he was failing in his marriage vows he made to you nearly sixty years before.

Do you remember the day you nearly gave Grandma and Auntie simultaneous heart attacks? I was in my teens, still the era of 'shot-gun' weddings when pregnant, single girls 'had' to get married. You expressed the opinion you didn't think it was right to 'force' sixteen-year-old girls into marriage. 'Why not let them have their babies and keep them, maintaining their friendship with the boy and if they want to get married later they can.' Auntie and Grandma were mortified or horrified or maybe both. But you didn't change your opinion. 'The girls and boys need support but enforcing marriage isn't necessarily the right thing to do.'

I'm about to write the stories of your maternal Grandma, but I'm not sure you will be pleased when I say your maternal Grandparents never married. Many years ago, I obtained your mother's birth certificate as a surprise for you. I discovered her birth is registered under her mother's maiden name with no father listed. I never did show you. But you found out when someone wrote a family history revealing the truth. 'It can't be true,' you told me. 'They wouldn't do that. They had eight children together. It's a mistake.'

You viewed your maternal Grandma and Mum from a child's point of view. Your Mum died when you were ten and you saw your Grandma very rarely, with little contact, after your dad moved back to Warracknabeal. Your relationships with your Grandma and Mum never developed beyond those early years. You loved and trusted them and in the way of a child they could do no wrong. By the time I was in my teens you viewed the world in a very different way. Life experience had shaped your thinking, your values, your perceptions of the society in which you lived. You had the courage to express your opinions, to disagree, or rather to disobey society's expectation of what should be done with pregnant teenage girls and the boys who had fathered these children.

'When I was a child, I spoke as a child, I understood as a child, I thought as a child: but when I became a man, I put away childish things.' (1 Corinthians 13:11). You were talking as a mature woman, Mum, when you considered the support pregnant girls needed. When you refused to accept your maternal grandparents had never married you were still cocooned in a ten-year-old's perception. In the death of your mother and the loss of close contact with your Grandma there had been no opportunity for these relationships to develop and mature. No opportunity for you to discover the layers of living in the lives of your mum and grandma, no opportunities for you to discover the layers in the stories you wanted me to tell.

8 . Alice Clark (Smart)

I hope I can write the layers on the page to honour your grandma as you trusted me to do. Who had the resilience to laugh as you bottle fed a pet lamb and an adult dog while your mum and her siblings, breathed with TB riddled lungs. A wise grandma creating memories of laughter amidst the reality of fast-approaching death.

Love, Judith

*

Of all the people who loved and cared for my mum during her childhood, of all the people who empathised with her in the years of her mother's struggle with TB it was her Grandma Alice who truly understood what Mum was going through. Until you walk a mile in another's shoes, until you can see the world through their eyes, you cannot truly understand the depth of what they are feeling or what it is they are feeling. It was as if Mum and her grandma were sharing the same pair of shoes so much of Mum's first ten years mirrored her Grandma's.

There's a risk in telling another's story especially when the story has been passed down. Four people may witness an accident. Their accounts of the accident may differ according to where they were standing and at what stage they became aware an accident was about to happen or had occurred. Did they know the victims of the accident or were they strangers? The witnesses may tell their family about the accident. What they tell adults will contain more graphic detail than what they will tell a six-year-old child. Their family may tell others. Each version contains the truth but how it is expressed will vary with the individual. If you ask each of the witnesses and those they told to retell the story thirty years later the story will vary again according to life experiences since the event. Those no longer children will still perceive much of the story through a child's eyes as they were at the time of the accident.

Great Grandma Alice was born at Phillip Flat outside Ararat on the 8th March 1877, one of eight children born to Phoebe and Eli. Phoebe died on 13th January 1887, eight weeks before Alice's tenth birthday. Phoebe died from TB. She had been sick for four years.

Prior to and after her mother's death Alice was aware of the deaths of several of her mother's siblings from TB and of her own siblings in the years to come. I'm not sure who cared for the children following Phoebe's death. It was rare for a dad to raise young children alone. In her role as a mum Alice gathered her children to her in sickness and in health. Was this in response to being gathered in when her mother died? Or was she trying to give her children the mother's love she missed when her mum died?

How did Great Grandma Alice find the strength, the stamina, the courage and resilience to care for her adult children with a TB diagnosis when in her experience such a diagnosis was a death sentence? Faced with the enormity of caring for two or three at the same time she still had the patience and motivation to create warm wonderful memories for my mum. 'Tell the story of my grandma and my mum,' my mum said. But what stories? All I have are tiny snippets, taking the cow to the common each day, bottle feeding the lamb and a jealous pet dog, the long walk to school alone 'because Grandma had to care for the sick ones'. Mum's memories were so rich and vital but the stories so miniscule. Is that the significance? Her grandma didn't have time to sit and play with Mum, so Mum was included in what was happening, the everyday chores. She still had her doll and a chair for her doll, there were cousins close by, the children down the street who were the children of the man who had been engaged to the Auntie she never knew, her mother's sister, the first one to die of TB after the grandpa she didn't know had died from TB. Mum knew all that. She went with her grandma to the cemetery on a regular basis to put flowers on the graves, an increasing number of graves.

What jobs did Grandma Alice have when she left school? I don't know. What hobbies did Grandma Alice have? I don't know. Did she read? If she did, what did she read? I don't know. She must have written letters because I know she wrote to Allie when Allie worked at various places beyond home as a domestic servant. Amongst Mum's few treasures are photo cards from Great Grandma Alice's sisters of their children. She obviously kept in touch with her siblings. Mum knew the names of Grandma Alice's siblings and where some of them lived. Was it Grandma Alice who told her? I don't know.

The hardest part of writing about my great grandmas is that the stories my parents told me have been from their perspective as a child.

There are many layers to any individual's life. A child's perspective is limited by their own life experience.

Often we talk of the visual or auditory triggering memory, but I believe the sense of smell can be an extremely powerful trigger too. One morning, in my first year at Melbourne Kindergarten Teachers College in Kew, I was waiting with a group of girls, all country students, for the pedestrian lights at Kew Junction. A heavily laden truck grunted through the intersection. We were busy chatting and taking little notice of the traffic but suddenly each one of us spun in the direction of the truck inhaling deeply. Above the smells of vehicle fumes and bitumen roads the perfume of sweet-smelling hay overwhelmed us. 'It smells like home,' someone said. We all nodded.

When I look at the two grainy photos of my mum feeding a lamb and a jealous dog it isn't just what I see, I can smell the pungent odour of chook manure and lamb manure. These smells never disgust me, they are part of farm life, just as the grit of summer dust and the tang of rain on dry earth are imprinted on my memory. Great Grandma Alice was a farm girl, these smells would have been imprinted on her memory as they are on mine. Mum was a town girl until she married Dad but living in a small town such smells would have been familiar to her too.

If I gently peel away the layers of these photos, I reveal the essence of Great Grandma's resilience, the values she lived by. Great Grandma was obviously a practical woman. When she lived at Reedy Creek (about eighteen kilometres from Broadford) with her husband Richard and their children they lived in a house made of 'bits and pieces'. In a small book *Nostalgia Reedy Creek*, former residents remember the family, 'Dick was a master rabbit-trapper. He did other work as it was available – a bit of mining sometimes.' Another recalls, 'He used to pull out any teeth needing attention with a pair of pliers giving the patient a sip of brandy later.' (I'm a teetotaller but I strongly believe if anyone was going to pull out my tooth with a pair of pliers, I'd need the sip of brandy before it was done not after and I don't think a sip would be sufficient!)

The family was obviously not wealthy and the area itself though strong on community spirit was not one of mansions and luxury gardens. Alice, to keep her family fed and clothed would have needed all her practical skills to do so. Sometime about 1920 they moved into

Broadford to live. I think they bought the house. Alice and Richard's youngest child Jean said, 'We never had much but we were a happy family.'

Sadness and death were not hidden from Mum during her Broadford visits, but I sense much laughter as well. Great Grandma knew much sadness, but her living was not consumed by the sadness. Amidst the busyness of caring for adult children with TB, caring for a small child who was visiting her mum, she had no problem with the child feeding a jealous dog. This was not a one-off event it was an ongoing event each time the lamb was fed. If I'm peeling the layers of the photos correctly, interpreting what I'm exposing correctly, Great Grandma was accepting there was much in the big picture of her life she couldn't change but in her ordinary, everyday existence there was much she could do to create a life worth living for herself and those around her. She couldn't change her mother's death, the deaths of her mother's siblings, the death of her own siblings, TB was the scourge of her family for generations, but she couldn't change that. She could however care for her adult children, she could care for her granddaughter who was experiencing exactly what she had experienced as little girl, she could laugh at the ridiculous, teach her granddaughter to laugh when surrounded by sadness. I'm not sure if Great Grandma was religious or not but as the smells of chook and lamb manure drift from the photos, the sound of lamb and dog slurping from the teat of the bottle and the laughter of a young girl mingled with the laughter of her grandma and the photographer ride the air currents into the rooms of those with lungs heavy with mucous I think of the saying, 'God grant me the serenity to accept the things I cannot change, courage to change the things I can and the wisdom to know the difference'.

Great Grandma was not an angelic woman. She was forthright with strong opinions. These are not Mum's memories but those of others who knew her when she was an older woman being cared for by her youngest daughter, herself a married woman with children. Her youngest daughter was the sixth of the eight adult children to be diagnosed with TB. But this was several years after the fifth had died and been buried. In this time medical research had progressed with antibiotics and treatment ensuring TB was not a death sentence.

Great Grandma Alice and Great Grandpa Richard never married. Their first two children have a vacant column on their birth certificates where the father's name should be listed. The two children are registered under their mother's maiden name. Recent DNA tests have proved Richard's paternity. I'm assuming it was after the first two Alice and Richard lived as husband and wife. Alice took Richard's surname and he was listed as the father on the subsequent children's birth certificates. Richard was already married to someone else. Three children of his first wife carry the Smart surname. The first child appears to be Richard's. The next two may carry his name but most likely not his DNA. There are layers to everyone's story, some layers kept hidden, kept secret, eventually revealed. In the telling we can assume much but unless we have walked a mile in their shoes, we do not know the story. The stories Mum wanted me to tell will be different to those of Great Grandpa's other family. We are connected, interconnected yet disconnected. The complexity of relationships and the decisions individuals make affect not only those involved at the time but through the generations. Alice and Richard lived outside the conventions of their time. Their decisions possibly causing hurt to others, or perhaps the decisions of others caused them hurt. The disintegration of relationships is rarely simple. Looking back, as I am, I cannot discern why, merely record it happened.

I met Great Grandma Alice once when I was about three-years old. I'm not sure if I remember meeting her or if I've been told the story so many times it has become my memory. I have a vague image of a kitchen I'm not familiar with and a lady I don't know smiling at me. The image is distant. I cannot bring it into focus.

I'm glad I met Great Grandma Alice. For the pleasure it gave my mum, for the pleasure it gave Great Grandma Alice. Whether my memory of the visit is real or imprinted by the retold story I'm glad I felt the warmth of her hug.

9
Catherine (Kate) Creswick (Jefferies)
(1866 - 1949)

St Arnaud, Kate's birth town, was a feisty little town. City based town planners designated a particular spot for the site of the town. The residents didn't agree. They chose their own site which is exactly where the current township of St Arnaud is today. Perhaps a feisty little town suited Kate's parents, Yorkshireman William and Irish Mary. They had eleven children. Like many families of the mid-1800s four of their children were interred in the local cemetery many years before they were. On leaving school Kate worked for a local family, possibly the Moggs whose name you will find in history books. When she informed them she was going to get married they urged her to reconsider. Apparently, they didn't want to lose her as she was very good with the children. Kate didn't reconsider or maybe she did out of courtesy but still made the same choice. She married her William. The Moggs family accepted her decision giving her a dress to be married in. It looks a splendid dress in the formal photos.

9. Catherine (Kate) Creswick (Jefferies)

Catherine, or Kate, as it seems she was always known was not famous or infamous. She was born in St Arnaud in 1866 where she stayed until she married William in 1889 when she moved to another small country town (Warracknabeal) where she lived until her death in 1949. Other than official Government records a researcher is unlikely to find Kate's name.

As I gathered the stories of my female forebears I realised how lucky I am to have so many stories of those who live on, in me. I also realised the laughter connecting not only the stories but the way the stories connected the family within each generation, the chuckles, the giggles and the belly-laughs passing on not only the stories but the humanness of those who shared the laughter.

Kate was a storyteller, as was her mother before her, and as was one of her sons, Fergus. Kate's mother Mary gathered her family around her entertaining them with stories of Ireland. Kate gathered her family of six children (although two died too young to enjoy the experience of their mother's stories) around her entertaining them with the stories of Ireland her mother had told her. You couldn't capture the gathering in a photo. A photo is static. These would have been noisy gatherings, 'tell us the one about', tell us when', 'what about the day' the joy, delight and richness of stories repeated of a far-away place none of them would ever physically visit but lived in their imaginations. Family stories are made for repetition. The listener often laughing before the story is finished for they know the ending. The listener begging to hear familiar stories for the stories keep alive the essence of those no longer in our physical presence. In such gatherings the participants are not neatly arranged on chairs they are scrunched together, physically connected, children on adult knees, adults so close they blend into a large mass bubbling with joy, anticipation, memories and the sheer pleasure of belonging. I heard many of these stories as we dawdled over a meal, food scraps drying on yet-to-be-washed plates, but no one caring, as stories leap-frogged from one to another, each story triggering another. Other times on Sunday afternoons as we visited elderly relatives the story telling starting again, the familiar repeated as I waited for the smile or eye-sparkle of the elderly as yesterday came alive again for them, as Mum and Dad smiled in delight to see those they loved seem young again for the afternoon. I didn't know it then how I was being wrapped in stories that would keep me warm when the teller was no longer with us.

Kate's washing board hangs in my laundry. To be quite honest I think Kate would laugh out loud to see the well-worn, singed-by-the-copper washing board hanging there. 'What have you got that thing for,' I can almost hear her say. I remember the day I asked Auntie if I could have it. No one else wanted it. It's destination was the local tip. Auntie handed it to me. 'It was my mother's,' she said. For me, it isn't a symbol of women's relegation to domestic chores, it is a reminder of my Great Grandma Kate. An ordinary woman doing ordinary things but it isn't her ordinariness I remember.

Great Grandma Kate was a gatherer of people. She gathered her children to her telling stories her mother told her, she gathered her younger siblings to their home when her mother died, she gathered her father-in-law to their home understanding his grief in the committal of his wife to a lunatic asylum, she gathered family friends to their home when times were tough, she gathered her eighteen month old granddaughter in when her mother was diagnosed with TB, Auntie ran her dressmaking business from the house, she gathered in William's nephew and cousin when they migrated from England and called in to spend time with them. Their home was a two-bedroomed timber cottage William built himself. He added a sleep-out as the family grew where the boys slept. He built a separate room in the back yard, optimistically called the Chalet. I knew it as a storage room but I guess it was also sleeping quarters. The small kitchen held a table which must have been 'cosy' at meal times when everyone was there. In all the stories I've heard never once did I hear anyone complain because the house was too small.

Great Grandma Kate gathered in those who were distant and those who had died. In the lounge room she hung three framed photos – her father-in-law Robert and Robert's two daughters (William's sisters), Ada and Amelia. Ada died aged 21 years. Amelia married and lived in Western Australia. About 1900 Robert went to Western Australia to live with Amelia and her family. The photos hung in the lounge room until the cottage was pulled down in the 1970's. William's family may have been scattered but Kate kept them close. Kate gathered in William's Mum who spent the last fourteen years of her life in Aradale, a lunatic asylum. She died there in 1891. Many families lose

9. Catherine (Kate) Creswick (Jefferies)

track of an ancestor committed to an asylum. Kate ensured Eliza was not lost, not her or her story. There was no shame in Eliza's illness. Kate's children and their children's children knew the story. Knew about Eliza's illness and Robert's sadness that never left him at having to make the choice he made. 'He was never the same again after committing Eliza'.

Great Grandma Kate had a sense of the ridiculous. She saw no problem in organising a formal photo shoot at the local photographers, Discaciati, of two of her sons with their pet sheep. The photographer's studio was up stairs. I wondered how they managed to get the partly grown sheep up the stairs. 'The sheep would follow the boys anywhere so it just followed them up the stairs and down again.' Auntie said. I can hear the hooves clacking and clattering on the stairs, the same stairs brides in their wedding day attire would ascend and descend, sense the photographer's amusement and the look of pride on the faces of two small boys. Kate had regular photos taken of her daughter particularly but also of the family. When the family scattered as families do she kept them close with her photographs.

Kate and William were both Australian born of migrant parents. There is a family story my maternal Grandpa, with the given names of Robert State was named Robert after his paternal grandfather and State because he was the first male child born after Federation. Federation came into being on 1st January 1901. My maternal Grandpa was born September 12 1901. He was the first of Kate and William's children to be born following Federation. Is this the basis of the family story? Whatever the story is based upon the significance is the importance of Federation to Kate and William. So significant they included the name State as part of my Grandpa's name. When their last child was born in 1905 her given names were Annie Beatrice Victoria. Kate and William named each of their children after family members but the Victoria was not after a family member. I always assumed it was after Queen Victoria but I suspect it was after the state in which Kate and William lived.

Amongst Auntie's possessions was a photo album, its pages now falling apart the photos set free from their place in the pages. The photos are all small, some studio portraits others personal camera shots. I always assumed it was Auntie's album but I'm beginning to suspect it may have been Kate's. The photos in excellent condition, some of the photos are named, e.g. Mrs Jones (who was Mrs Jones?) others I have no clue as to who they are. Nevertheless, I've kept the album, maybe one day I'll meet someone who can name them, someone who can help me discover their story, their place in Kate's story.

I look at the many photo albums lined up on my bookshelf. I remember the number of times Mum went through the many photos she kept safely in calico bags. We learn many things in our growing up, some we are aware of, others we aren't until one day we realise who we inherited a habit from. Sometimes as I share stories and laughter with my scrapbooking friends as we adhere photos to the page and journal the story the photo tells I think of Kate and how she would have loved to belong to such a group.

Kate's husband William suffered a stroke two or three years before he died. It meant the end of his working life but he now had plenty of time to go fishing. One day he arrived home from a fishing trip to the creek soaking wet and accompanied by a man equally wet who had pulled him out of the creek when he slipped in. Apparently William was in no danger of drowning but the stroke had limited his capacity to climb out. I rather think Mum, who told me the story found it a little amusing but her Grandmother was naturally concerned next time William slipped the story may not have such a happy ending. 'You're not allowed to go to the creek by yourself anymore,' Kate informed William. 'You always have to have someone with you.' I gather William obeyed his wife's orders. 'I think Grandma always listened to Grandpa,' Mum said, 'But …' she never finished the sentence. I suspect Kate may have always listened to her husband but made up her own mind about the correct course of action.

At some stage in Kate's life she had to get false teeth. She didn't like wearing them because they hurt. Even for a photo on the day Kate and William celebrated their fiftieth wedding anniversary Kate wouldn't wear her false teeth. Mum always laughed when she looked at the photo. 'She wouldn't wear them,' Mum said. 'she absolutely refused to wear them.' Then she'd smile quietly murmuring to me, 'she could be quite determined.' An acknowledgement between the two us that perhaps we had inherited just a little of Kate's determination!

In Kate's last few months she was bedridden, cared for at home by Auntie. Mum was still living there but working full time although she helped out before and after work. Kate decided Mum was to make her hot chocolate each night. Mum was glad to do this but on occasions Auntie would do it. 'She always knew,' Mum laughed. 'I don't know how she did, but she always knew and she'd complain.' I'd laugh at the story with Mum. 'Bonnie didn't make this,' she'd say. 'Bonnie didn't make this. I can tell the difference.' Sadness may have shaken the foundations of the little cottage at times but I think laughter helped strengthen them.

When I want to lose myself in a good book, creating an uninterrupted space I sit in Kate's rocking chair, (a gift from her father-in-law Robert in 1895), gently rock and read, the stories enmeshed in the still supple springs cocooning me. It was Kate's chair, her storytelling chair, her chair she sat in to feed her babies, to rock a fractious child to sleep, a chair she relaxed in, a chair in a set place near the fire in her kitchen where she read the letters from family and friends. When I was a little girl I rocked gently, 'it's old so be gentle' I was told as I rock gently now because now it is really old. Our sons learnt to rock gently respecting the old rocking chair. I sensed the stories then as I do now, could feel them curl up from the springs, the timbers firm with the strength of the stories. Great Grandma died three years before I was born. When I rock in the rocking chair sometimes, I'm a little girl sitting on her knee being cuddled and rocked, sometimes I'm drifting close to the family circle as Great Grandma tells her stories and sometimes when life hits a rough patch, I feel her drawing me in.

Dear Mum,

You had two rather strong-willed Grandmas, didn't you? Two strong-willed but family-orientated women. I often thought you were family-orientated because you lost your mum when you were so young. Perhaps that coloured your choices too, but with an upbringing strongly influenced by both grandmas and witnessing their commitment not only to their children but their extended family, it becomes clear your childhood life-experiences were a major factor in your focus on family.

My childhood life-experiences, though different to yours in many respects, were lived within extended family too. Auntie, Grandma and Grandpa, Grandpa Bob and Grandma Jessie were not just names but people we visited or visited us on a very regular basis for we all lived within the

Warracknabeal area. They were not just special occasion visits. Your half-brother Bill and his wife Faye were part of our family circle. Your half-sister Betty and her husband Jim and their children were not so geographically close, but you still cared about and were interested in their family happenings. You were Auntie Bonnie and Uncle Stan to their children. Dad's brother, his wife and their two children lived locally too. The visits were frequent.

When life became a struggle in your later years my automatic response was to be there for you and Dad. I travelled many kilometres in those years but as the world diminished for you it was family you clung to. I came willingly, not out of a sense of duty but an inherited sense of family-orientated love.

Perhaps it may be unwise to let Dad and Michael read this letter as I talk of strong-willed grandmas. They are sure to make some remark, similar to what they have said in the past, implying you and I are stubborn. We disagreed, preferring the word determined!

Love, Judith

10
Amy Boon (Hancock)
1865 - 1939

As I attempt to give voice to my female forebears the Irish proverb: 'We live in the shelter of one another' keeps weaving through each story. The way the stories of each generation of women physically connect, the way the generations interconnect is rather like the warp and weft of woven cloth. The individual threads have their own strengths, but it is in the weaving of the cloth the texture becomes obvious. Not one of these stories could be told without another. The generations of my female forebears may go back to the beginning of time, but the cloth is still in production for the stories of those who come after me have yet to be lived. And me?

When I first began I saw myself as the recorder, the gatherer of the stories of resilient women who faced adversity in its various forms but through a sense of connection, of belonging, having others to support them, to understand their adversity and to share with them they found the path of living again. I failed to realise I too am an intrinsic part of that cloth. When my world goes 'belly up' none of my female forebears are alive today but the very fact they too have experienced 'belly up' moments creates a sense of not feeling alone.

Great Grandma Amy, a strong-willed rather feisty individual was part of a large family community. She was not consumed or lost within the numbers but connected within the extended family.

When my dad was a young boy, each Sunday after worship at the Methodist Church family members would gather at Amy's house for a shared meal. The adults would then sit inside talking while Dad and his cousins played outside. Just before three the cousins would walk down to the Church to attend Sunday School. The older cousins ensuring the younger cousins arrived safely. In one family snapshot with all the cousins present Dad is looking decidedly grumpy. I asked him did he remember why. 'We had a game of football to play,' he replied indignantly, 'and we had to stop to have our photo taken.'

Amy was born in Clunes as was her husband James. In the mid-1870s the families moved to Avon Plains outside Donald. Gold may have been the original lure for Amy and James parents to Clunes but farm land was their reason for choosing Avon Plains. Amy's dad named his property Modbury after the place of his birth in Devon, England. A number of years ago Dad drove me past the farm. It still carries the Modbury name. Amy and James married at Avon Plains and were part of a family company created by James' dad.

My Grandma, born at Avon Plains was Amy and James' first child. Their next six children were born in Maryborough or St Arnaud. I often wondered why as their home was Avon Plains. I haven't discovered where all the extended family lived but possibly as Amy's time drew near, she would stay with family who would assist with the birth and care for Amy and her newborn. Amy and James' eighth child was born in Warracknabeal.

In time Amy and James wanted to go it alone moving to farmland at Aubrey, twenty miles beyond Warracknabeal with their young family. They added to their family after their arrival and had eight children. They also included one of James' nephews, Albert, in their family home. Albert's mother died leaving her husband with four young children. Amy and James, with their own small children, did not hesitate to take ten-year-old Albert into their home and raise him with their own. Albert stayed with the family through his childhood remaining with the family working Amy and James' farm until he enlisted in WWI. He never lost contact with his dad or his sisters.

Amy and James may have been geographically separated from their families and independent but family ties were never severed. Visits were regular between Aubrey and Donald, Avon Plains, St Arnaud and Maryborough for these were all towns and surrounding areas individual members flexing their wings moved to. When Dad drove me around the only map he needed was imprinted on his mind he had visited so often. Family snapshots show the visits were not occasional ones. These were not formal 'smile on cue' photos rather the sort where some are laughing, others ready to laugh and some finished their laughter. It appears many were taken at the same place as the same lattice work is in many photos possibly where his great grandma lived with family. She died in 1934, aged ninety-three, nearly seven years after Dad was born.

I often think of the many trips Amy and James and my grandparents with Dad and his brother made to the family. Initially the trips would have been long, slow plodding trips in horse drawn conveyances. During WWI Amy and James bought a car. The trips would have been quicker and more comfortable along the familiar roads. Today, as I travel the same familiar roads the stories Dad told me resurface as I pass landmarks triggering one of Dad's stories in my memory bank.

Amy and James' world was never the same, ever again, nor for the rest of the family either, with the advent of WWI. Albert Leslie, known by the family as Les, was the first to enlist. He was studying to be a Methodist Minister at the time. 'I cannot expect others to enlist if I am unwilling to do so myself,' he said. He died two days before his 25th birthday in 1916. His name is on the Arras Memorial for the Missing. Albert John (James' nephew) brought up with Amy and James' children enlisted as did one of their other sons, Arthur James. Albert died in 1917 two days after their son Arthur James died in action. Albert and Arthur's names are on the Menin Gate Memorial for the Missing.

Amy told one of her granddaughters when they got the 'Missing in Action' telegrams she couldn't sleep. She imagined each one lying injured, in agony, with no one knowing where they were, unable to find them or unable to reach them. When the telegrams arrived with the dreaded news 'Killed in Action', she slept. Nothing more could be done. They would never come home.

When 'the three boys', as they are still known, died, Amy and James grieved in a community with so many grieving for young men who would never come home. Individual and community grief, individual and family grief, Amy and James remained active in the community continuing to donate to various war causes, continuing to serve on farming committees but their sadness never went away. Their single daughters, still at home, were part of community activities providing recitations and singing. Their daughter Alice, my grandma, married in March 1914 at the small Methodist Church close to the family farm, before war was declared. Another daughter Beatrice married in 1918. In respect for the grief they all still felt it was a family wedding at home. Life would never be the same again, but they found space in their grief for hope. Family, community and church, Amy and James were connected and interconnected with others who knew 'the three boys', who grieved with them, as they grieved with others experiencing sorrow as they were.

James died suddenly eight years after WWI ended. He never stopped searching for information about the deaths of the three boys – how, where, when – until the military authorities were able to answer his questions.

The one consistent family story is in relation to how James and Amy were informed of the death of one of their sons – possibly Albert Leslie. The family farm was twenty miles out of town. The Postmaster waited until James and Amy were in town doing their shopping, as he knew they eventually would. Once he saw James, he picked the telegram off the shelf, walked out into the street and in full view of the public handed James the telegram telling him his son was dead. The grief for the three boys has been handed from one generation to another. The anger and indignity, the lack of compassion and respect in the way James was given the telegram has been handed from one generation to another. 'Grandpa never recovered from that,' my dad told me. He died before my dad was born.

A couple of years ago my husband and I visited France and Ypres to see the names of the three boys on the Arras and Menin Gate Memorials to the Missing. I was surprised at the intensity of my grief for three young men I had never known. Viewing the thousands upon thousands of names of the Missing at both Memorials is overwhelming and overpowering. I left a poppy for each of the boys. They are not forgotten. I have not inherited the intensity of the sadness but the sadness never goes away. Our guide for our Battlefields Tour said there are plans to build another Memorial for the Missing in Arras where every name of all those missing in WWI will be listed. There will be no rank, no nationality, no 'side' fought for, just the names of the missing. I rather think our Albert Leslie would like that. I rather think the whole family would be in favour of such a memorial. Whatever language a family spoke, whatever country they called home, whatever political ideology they fought for, it would become a shared grief – a community sorrow. The sadness never goes away for either side. Never-ending sadness is the price of war.

Amidst Mum and Dad's collection of family photos is one of Amy and James with some of their children and their partners. On the back is a letter. 'That's Grandma's writing,' my dad said. 'I remember her writing.' (His grandma died when he was eleven.) The letter on the back was written to Albert. It was about the ordinary, the mundane, the everyday, who had taken the photo, their new camera and how they'd send some more another time. The letter was posted. Albert was killed in action three days later. The letter returned to Amy and James.

Amy died in January 1939. Dad was going on a holiday with his mum to a guest house in Portland. Amy, recovering from major surgery wanted to go. Dad's mum didn't think her mother was strong enough. 'What Grandma wanted Grandma got,' Dad said. Even an eleven-year-old boy understood determination. He was sharing a room with his grandma and woke up in the night with his grandma trying to pull the blankets off his bed because she was cold. Amy had either fallen out of bed or collapsed on the floor after getting out of bed. She was cold and wanted Dad's blankets to keep warm. His mum heard their voices and came running. Amy died later that night. Amy's son and one of her daughters arrived down in Portland the next day. Amy's body returned to Warracknabeal for burial with James. 'Mum had a tough time of it that night,' my dad said. 'The guest house owner didn't like being woken up for Mum to get a doctor then she didn't like being woken up again so Mum could ring home.'

Dad had strong memories of women who could care for themselves. No wonder when I left home his one piece of advice ensured I could take care of myself.

11
Charlotte Chamberlain (Avery)
1855 – 1924

The blue sky was as highly polished as Charlotte's silver when demurely dressed twelve-year-old Pat, accessorised with her white gloves, attended her first ladies afternoon tea at her Grandma Charlotte's home. Charlotte regularly hosted afternoon teas and today was Pat's initiation into this female ritual. Unfortunately, she was a little distracted by a dog peering in the window desperate for someone to come and play with it. But ladies, or white-glove-wearing-young-girls learning to be ladies, did not play with dogs. Pat knew remaining seated was expected of her. Several decades later the disappointment of missing out on playing with the dog had not diminished.

Charlotte's afternoon teas figured strongly in the memory of one of her grandsons too. Jack's dad died when Jack was still very young. His mother, with five young children to bring up alone sold their farm after her husband's death buying a house behind her parent's home in Dimboola. Ettie usually helped with food for her mother's afternoon teas. Carefully removing the freshly baked biscuits from the oven she placed them on the bench to cool. A clean tea towel covering the biscuits may have kept the flies at bay but it did not deter one small boy named Jack from sampling one then two and many more. When Ettie returned to the kitchen the tray was empty. Jack was not specific about the punishment his grandma administered but like Pat, several decades later his memory of the event had not diminished.

My dad didn't know his Grandma Charlotte. She died nearly three years before he was born. His older cousins, however, were eager to share their stories of Charlotte. 'Apparently she was quite a formidable woman,' he told me on many occasions. Although he did say his mother got on okay with her mother-in-law Charlotte. Then he'd laugh, 'But Mum didn't argue with her.'

I have one photo of Charlotte and I must admit she does look somewhat formidable, although photos can be deceiving. My paternal grandma looks severe and stern in her photos but all I remember is how good it felt when she put her arm around me each time I saw her.

Charlotte was born in Balhannah in the Adelaide Hills. Her parents migrated from England, both from the county of Wiltshire. Her husband William was also Australian born, both his parents from the county of Buckinghamshire. They too settled in the Adelaide hills.

Charlotte and William married on the 25th December 1873 'at the residence of the bride's father.'

The residence was a substantial wattle and daub hut on the family property at Wirrabara where Charlotte's father had selected land in the early 1870s. Charlotte's parents had a strong Christian faith as did William's parents. Until a church building was erected in Wirrabara, Church services were held at their home. It was a twenty-five-mile horseback ride from Melrose for the Minister to officiate at the wedding ceremony presumably as part of the Christmas Day service.

Charlotte and William's first home was a two-roomed stone cottage on the property William had selected at Caltowie outside Jamestown. Their nine children were born at this home. Two of the children died there and were buried in the Jamestown cemetery.

There are many risks in gathering the stories of those I never met. Dad retold the stories of Grandma Charlotte whom he had never met. These were stories told by his cousins who only knew the older Charlotte. Dad's mother only knew Charlotte in her adult years. There was one instance, however, when my paternal grandpa gave a hint of the type of mother Charlotte had been. It was in his later years when 'senile decay' started to claim his mind. He asked, 'When's

Mum coming?' My mum, sitting with him at the time, assumed he was talking about his wife, as he often referred to her as 'Mum'. She was in the kitchen at the time, so Mum replied, 'She won't be long'. Grandpa's face lit up like the summer sun. It was then my mum realised he was talking about his own mum, not his wife. The look was not of a small child afraid of a formidable woman, but a little boy filled with delight to see his mum. My mum felt a great sadness at the false hope she had given Grandpa but having similar experiences with Mum when she had dementia, I realised the joy was in the anticipation not the fulfilment of the promise, for the dementia mind soon forgets the question and the response.

In the approximately twenty-eight years Charlotte and William lived outside Jamestown they were involved in the community, church, school, William taking his turn as a councillor, active in the annual agricultural show. Some of William's brothers lived close by. In all of this it is William I read about. Even in birth announcements in the SA papers William is mentioned but Charlotte's name is not mentioned. She is merely 'the wife of'.

About 1900 Charlotte and William and their seven surviving children moved to Antwerp outside Dimboola. William and the three older boys each drove a team of horses pulling laden wagons from Jamestown to Murray Bridge, crossing the river on the punt then following the railway line to Dimboola before branching out to Antwerp. They then built a house for the family before Charlotte with the two younger boys and two girls joined them from Adelaide where they had been staying with family.

William was a Justice of the Peace and a magistrate in Dimboola. He was known for his fairness in judicial decisions. He faced some criticism over one of his decisions. Before him on one case was a white man and an Aboriginal man. The white man accused of assaulting the Aboriginal man. He found the white man guilty. Many in the community were horrified at the injustice, how could a white man be guilty? William looked at the facts not the colour of their skin. I may feel a sense of pride in William's attitude to the indigenous people, however it doesn't change the fact that William, like all other farmers, had claimed ownership of what was traditional Aboriginal land.

Whatever layer of story I peel away in relation to Charlotte, family and community are always present. Life would have been tough but always family and community were there. In new places she was part of the development of community. Men had jobs to do, they interacted with other men who perhaps worked the farm with them or neighbours. Women were more isolated, they understood the need for women to create community, to be there when children were unwell, or they were in childbirth. Charlotte was part of all this, but like the other wives she was in the background. The afternoon teas she hosted in Dimboola reflected her responsibilities as the wife of a man in William's position. But they were also essential to the community of women supporting one another. Pat may have complained about white gloves and sitting at afternoon tea when she'd rather be playing with a dog. It may have been seen as an initiation into the world of women and their place in society but more importantly it was an initiation into the importance of women being with other women, the importance of the community of women.

Charlotte scares me. Strong-willed, forthright, she obviously had expectations how others should behave, how her grandchildren should behave and apparently not afraid to express her opinions or administer punishment. But I'm not quite ready to stop picking at the layers of Charlotte's story just yet. There's another story niggling at the back of my mind.

William, as I've said, was a just man. He planned how he would provide equally for his sons with land as each son married and his daughters with money and chattels after both parents died. William died first. The plans he set in place to provide for his wife were respected and carried out. Charlotte's will reflected a continuance of these plans. Except as she aged, becoming frailer, not as formidable, one daughter convinced Charlotte to leave everything to her and nothing to her sister. Well, that is the story passed down. I'm not so afraid of Charlotte now. I'm reminded of how vulnerable the elderly are. Even when they know it shouldn't be done, that it isn't right, sometimes the elderly cannot fight any more. Charlotte and my dad, Grandma and Grandson, vulnerable and elderly, knew what was happening but had lost the ability to fight. There are imperfections in family relationships, imperfections in people, greed, arrogance, lack of care about others. Do we hide the stories, or is the strength of the story in the connection of others at another time feeling a sense of belonging when coping with the unfairness within families and community?

Dad always wanted to show my brother and myself where his grandparents had settled in Jamestown and his great grandparents had settled in Wirrabara. We went on a road trip. I stood at the window of the now ruined house William had built for Charlotte and himself – their first home – only the walls remain. I stood at the window space gazing down the conifer lined entrance to the farm. I'm sure Charlotte was standing beside me. How often did she look down that driveway waiting for William and his brother to return from Broken Hill where they had taken salted meat to sell to the miners? How many days were they away? She'd know when they were due back. How often did she glance down the driveway peering up the road she knew they'd come along, waiting, praying, urging their safe return until she saw the dust announcing their arrival long before they turned in the gate. Did she wave from the window welcoming them home? Or didn't ladies do that? The children probably ran to greet their dad.

Charlotte's formidableness is diminishing.

In 1902 Charlotte's dad, now a widower, decided to return to England for a holiday to see his brothers. He caught the train from Adelaide to Melbourne to board the ship to England. Charlotte and William made the 20-mile trip into Dimboola from their home in Antwerp by horse and wagon for the ten minutes the train stopped at the Dimboola station. Charlotte would have been glad they did this. Her dad died in Glasgow. Accidental death the coroner said. Murder the family said. We'll never know the true story about his death but I'm absolutely sure Charlotte, until the day she died, treasured those final ten minutes she had with her dad.

Another of Charlotte and William's children was diagnosed with diphtheria. 'Take him home and love him as much as possible,' the doctor said, 'for he will die.' Charlotte took him home. As the mucous coating on his throat became thicker and thicker, as his little lungs struggled for air Charlotte grabbed the bottle brush from the kitchen and scrubbed and scrubbed and scrubbed at his throat until it was red raw. He lived to raise a family of his own.

Great Grandma Charlotte was indeed a most formidable woman.

11. Charlotte Chamberlain (Avery)

Dear Mum,

The autumn sun still held warmth as we stood in the Jamestown cemetery. The unmarked grave in front of us held the remains of John and Ida, the two infant children of Charlotte and William. 'I wonder how Charlotte felt leaving these two little ones behind when they moved to Antwerp?' you murmured. I wasn't sure if you were asking me a question or merely making a statement. I had no answer. We could only assume how Charlotte may have felt. When I think of formidable Great Grandma Charlotte I always think of your murmured reflection, Mum. It reminds me of how you would quietly guide me to consider the many layers of those I met.

Like the time I was looking at one of Dad's school photos and made an unkind remark about the obviously several-sizes-too-small jumper one of the girls was wearing. You remarked, 'They were a large family and it was the depression.' I silently apologised to the girl for my remark. But you weren't guiding me that day at Jamestown cemetery, it was more a comment by one mother as to how another mother may have felt. You and I were fully aware of Charlotte's 'formidable woman' reputation but I think we each felt a little guilty for only considering that aspect of who Charlotte was without the respecting the grief she must have felt on the children's deaths. Sometime in the darkest hours close to midnight on 26th October 1884 John drew his first breaths. Three hours later when night was still in its depth of darkness he died on 27th October 1884. John only knew darkness, he never had the chance to experience the light of sunrise or the lingering sunset. How formidable had Charlotte been that day? Ida was born on 14th November 1885. She lived for eighteen months until diphtheria claimed her on the 8th May 1887. 'A beautiful bud to bloom in heaven' were the words accompanying the death announcement in the paper. How formidable was Charlotte on that day?

Remember the first time you said to me, 'Your brother yells at me all the time', and I replied, 'we all yell at you Mum. You don't put your hearing aids in so we have to yell, and then one day you do put them in but we can't see them under your hair so we keep yelling. Then you get cross because we are yelling when we don't have to.' You just waved your hands at me in frustration. I'm sorry I let trust in my brother put your words down to dementia rather than hear your cry for help. I hadn't heard my brother yell at you, you and Dad never yelled at each other nor did you yell at us. You and Dad had disagreements, but they were never yelling matches. You chastised us but they were never yelling events. Dad was a decent, honourable and respectful person, he would never treat you aggressively nor allow anyone else to do so either. Then came that terrible day when I saw and heard my brother yelling at you, physically intimidating you, with Dad cringing and stepping backwards. I was a powerless witness.

How, I've wondered many, many, many times since that awful, awful day did this happen?

You and Dad were not controlling parents, it wasn't about having 'power' over my brother and me. There were rules and boundaries, but these were more guides than rigid fences. There were consequences for inappropriate actions, but these were always clearly defined. You treated each other with respect and talked through differences of opinion, you gave the same respect and talked through differences of opinion with my brother and me. Gender was never an issue.

When you and Dad had us baptised, you promised 'to bring us up in the way you would like us to follow.' It appeared my brother and I had chosen the paths you wished for us. You trusted both of us as we trusted you. As you and Dad aged, as dementia made you frail, as a heart condition and back problems made Dad frail, it appears my brother and his wife maintained an outwards appearance of doing the right thing by you both while using your vulnerability to not only gain power and control over you and your resources but to erode family relationships. Trust was always a protective roof over our family unit. The words and actions of my brother and his wife, however, were like white ants in the stumps supporting a house. By the time you and Dad realised, by the time I realised, the depth of the deceit, the white ants had already taken over. It was too late. Our family unit was destroyed.

For you and Dad trust was replaced by fear.

I could have fought for your rights Mum, but when I said you had to complain before I could do anything you were afraid, 'I have to do what your brother says or I can't see your father anymore. Your brother is in charge now. I have to do what he says.'

I had two Dads. The one when my brother and his wife were not present and he told me what he wanted to do. The other when they were present when he was too afraid to disagree with my brother. I fought for Dad's rights trying to protect his well-being and his financial resources but good does not always triumph over bad.

For me, trust was replaced by a sense of powerlessness. But as I struggled in this quagmire, I thought of Great Grandma Charlotte.

Love,

Judith

MY GREAT GREAT GRANDMAS

12
Phoebe Hall (Clarke)
1853 - 1887

In 1861, at seven years of age, Phoebe, along with most of her siblings was convicted of vagrancy and incarcerated in a Melbourne gaol for twelve months. The catalyst for such a conviction was the arrest of their mother Mary for shoplifting about four months after the death of their father. In an act of kindness, the judge convicted the young children so they could be with their mother as she served her sentence. Incarceration was hardly ideal but with no one else to care for the children the alternative was not particularly palatable either. The children and Mary were initially in the Gaol Camp (the permanent gaol in Ararat not completed until later in 1861) before being sent to a gaol in Melbourne.

Many of the stories of my great, great grandmas have been lost in the dust for each of them lived in rural Victoria or South Australia. Although each drew their last breath on Australian soil most drew their first breaths in Ireland, England or Cornwall. Phoebe was one of the two of my great, great grandmas who only ever breathed Australian air.

When stories are caught in the increasingly dusty landscape, as farmers cleared the trees holding the topsoil together, a family history researcher has trouble unearthing the facts.

Phoebe was born in 1853 in Cavendish, a small town about sixteen miles from Hamilton in western Victoria. Her birth, however, was registered in South Australia. Over several decades there were bureaucratic discussions concerning the exact placement of the invisible line marking the Victorian/South Australian border which means births, deaths and marriages were registered according to where the invisible line was at the time. I suspect Phoebe's birth was only registered because an 'official' visited the little town gathering such information for the records. I have been unable to find birth records for some of her siblings nor the death records of those siblings who died very young. Phoebe's parents, James and Mary, appear to have avoided contact with 'authority' figures. This may be due to the fact Mary was an ex-convict and James' arrival in Australia is clouded in mystery I have yet to solve. Did he come of his own free will or was the choice made by authority figures he chose to avoid?

Phoebe's dad was a timber sawyer. Cavendish, known as red gum country, was an obvious choice to settle for a time. The little town was home to a labouring community, many of whom were employed, as needed, by the owners of some of the large properties in the area.

By the time Phoebe's dad died in 1860 the family was living a few miles out of Ararat on the Port Fairy Road. The area they were living in is known for the quantity of timber felled on settlement. Eight children are listed on James death certificate between the ages of fifteen and one year of age. The cause of death is given as 'an abscess on the hand' but James actually died of a lung disease, possibly TB.

After their release from gaol, Mary and the children returned to Ararat, to the hut they left behind. I think it may have been on Crown Land. James had been running a sly grog shop there prior to his death. A timber sawyer by trade he would have been in no fit state to work as a sawyer when suffering the effects of TB. He could, however, make a living as a sly grog shop owner. Sly grog shops were unlicensed venues and the alcohol served of suspect quality. They were illegal but often in rural communities when law enforcement officers were working long hours over vast distances, they ignored those who weren't causing trouble. James and Mary weren't exactly conforming to the laws of the land.

In 1871 Phoebe married a local farmer, Eli Clark. They lived at Cathcart, just outside Ararat. Phoebe and Eli had eight children before Phoebe died of TB in 1887. Their last child was born the year before she died. He died soon after birth. Phoebe suffered from TB for four years before she died.

What do I know about Phoebe? She was a daughter, a sister, a granddaughter, a wife and a mother. She was one of at least thirteen children but when her mother died in 1894 only five were still living, TB claiming the lives of most of those who lived to adulthood. It would be very easy to add Phoebe's name to the list of family members dying from TB, and to the list of young mums leaving motherless children, to sigh and ponder the depth of grief for her immediate and extended family. To put a full stop at the end of the list as though it was the end of Phoebe's story. Phoebe may have died at the age of thirty-four years, but she lived those thirty-four years. She wasn't sitting down waiting to die.

Phoebe was born in Cavendish, a small town of labouring people, a community of people who made a living by hard work, a community of people who understood a life where money was hard to come by. If a sense of community was important, so too, was a strong sense of maintaining the family unit. Her dad died; the family unit remained intact. Her mum was arrested, through the kindness of the judge, aware of the family's plight the family unit remained intact. The eldest boy was not incarcerated, he kept the family hut ready for when they returned from the Melbourne Gaol. The family unit was complete once more. Phoebe married remaining in the local community where family contact was possible. Eli, her husband, was a local, his family were close by. Phoebe's brother John died in 1883 from TB. He was married with a young family and had had TB for ten years. On his death it was Phoebe who made the cemetery arrangements, perhaps paying for the plot he was buried in. Phoebe, a woman, made the arrangements. Phoebe, in many ways conforming to expectations of society had no qualms about doing what was considered a man's job in arranging for the burial of her brother, providing support to her sister-in-law at the same time. Phoebe died leaving seven living children. I'm not sure if Eli managed to keep the family unit intact after her death. I hope he did. Phoebe's mum kept her family unit intact, caring for each of her adult children as they succumbed to the dreaded TB.

Perhaps that is Phoebe's story, a lifetime sense of belonging, of community, of never feeling isolated. I could feel pity for Phoebe's thirty-four years of living but pity seems to create a shell of a woman, a woman on the edge of living. I don't see Phoebe as being on the edge of living. For thirty-four years, whatever craters in the road she had to negotiate she never had to do so alone. And when her brother died it was Phoebe, the daughter of a sly grog shop owner, the daughter of an ex-convict, Phoebe who had served time in gaol found guilty of vagrancy, illiterate Phoebe who did a man's job arranging the burial plot for her brother. From my perspective I see Phoebe, who would herself be dead in four years' time, as a resilient woman who saw a job that needed doing and did it.

When Phoebe's husband, Eli, died forty-five years after Phoebe, he was buried in the Ararat cemetery with his second wife. The remaining children of Eli and Phoebe put a notice in the paper at the time of his death, ending it with the words, 'Mum and Dad together again.'

*

Dear Mum,

Going to Church every Sunday was as natural as breathing for us. Sometimes on a Sunday afternoon I'd go to the little Anglican Church not far from our farm with Auntie. I think the services were only once a month. This was a treat, not a chore, getting dressed up in my 'going to Church' clothes on a Sunday afternoon as well as Sunday morning and going to a different Church without you and Dad was a grown-up thing to do. I recall the service was the same but different to our Methodist service.

Auntie was in many ways a fundamentalist, wasn't she? If the Bible said the world was created in seven days, then it was. Yet, she was open-minded in regard to the different denominations. Perhaps having a Catholic Irish grandmother, although she never knew her as she died before Auntie was born, influenced her thinking. Her maternal grandmother may have been Catholic, but her maternal grandfather was Church of England as were her paternal grandparents.

I keep coming back to the notion of what we learn may have a greater influence on us than we realise, than what we are taught. 'Do what I do not what I say.' I don't hear this very often now but in my growing up I seem to recall hearing it on a regular basis. Perhaps Auntie and my grandparents were of a generation more aware of children learning more than what they are taught. 'Give me a child for the first seven years and I'll give you a man.' This is a well-known Catholic saying acknowledging the significance of those first seven years of a child's life. Being a kindergarten teacher, I am well aware of the research reinforcing the importance of the first seven years of a child's life experience on their future development.

I remember being shocked with your response when I said I wanted to ask one of our neighbour's children, who I was friendly with, to come to our Sunday School concert. 'She probably wouldn't be allowed to come,' you said. 'Why?' I asked. 'Because Catholics aren't allowed to go to other Churches.' It was my first exposure to the Protestant-Catholic divide. The family were our neighbours, I played with their children, the dads helped each other out with farm stuff and the mums talked about things that mums talk about. What I had learnt from you and Dad was that being Catholic was just a label indicating you worshipped in another building. On that day however you taught me about the Catholic-Protestant divide. I thought it ridiculous as they were just ordinary people like us.

But going back to when I was even younger, when we lived in the town, the man next door to us was sent to prison for three months. The day he was sentenced you went next door to see his wife. 'But they're Catholic and he's just been sent to jail,' someone said to you. 'Then she needs a good neighbour,' you said and went to visit her. When the man came home again our neighbour asked Dad to pick him up from the station. They didn't have a car and she didn't want him to walk home through the town before he saw the family again. So Dad picked him up. Years and years later one of the man's daughters came to town to see where they used to live. Their house was no longer there. It had been burnt down. By sheer coincidence you and Dad built your retirement home there. Dad was able to talk to her and she told him of the life her mum and dad lived after they left Warracknabeal. You were in care by then Mum and past the stage of Dad being able to share this with you. But Dad was so pleased the family had been so happy. 'He was a decent man,' Dad said. 'He just made a mistake.' I know you would have been equally pleased Mum to know the family were so content and happy after their hiccup.

You weren't pleased the day you met a new minister who came to the Methodist Church though, were you? I'm sure you remember this story. Dad was to take him around to introduce him to the families in our area. Not just Methodist families but all families. As Dad finished getting ready the Minister asked you about the neighbours. You mentioned their names and the denomination each was associated with. You mentioned our closest neighbour, the Catholic ones! 'Well, we won't want to go there, will we?' This man of the cloth retorted. 'You couldn't ask for better neighbours,' you responded, a little sharply I suspect.

As the years ticked by the divide between Catholic and Protestant softened, and each was allowed to visit the other. You talked with our Catholic neighbour about this. Both of you agreed the division was unnecessary and had caused much hurt to some families. You commented you found the interior of the Catholic Church building rather ornate. Our neighbour commented she found the interior of the Methodist Church building quite plain. The two of you could discuss religion without a single cross word of disagreement.

You taught me lots of things Mum, but you didn't teach me respect for those of different denominations. I learnt that from the way you treated other people, the way you lived your life.

Love,

Judith

13
Jane Woodall (Smart)
1850 – 1935

A short clinical article in the *Pleasant Creek Advertiser* in 1864 informs the public: 'An inquest was held on Sunday last by the Coroner, J. G. Taylor Esq., on the body of a child fourteen-months old, the daughter of Mrs. Woodall residing at Opossum Gully.' It appeared the child had fallen into a waterhole on the Saturday and drowned. 'The evidence of a sister of the child, Jane Woodall, bears the closest on the case. 'On Saturday about two o'clock I went to look for my sister, having missed her; I was looking for her about a quarter of an hour; I heard my sister Mary Ann call me; I went and found her with the deceased; she said she found her in the waterhole and pulled her out, and laid her on the bank; I took her up and took her over to my brother, who was at the end of the dam digging; I then went for my mother who was at Mrs McKay's about half a mile off; I do not know how far the hole was from our house; it was not far.' The coroner would not take depositions from the child who found the body as she was too young to understand the nature of the oath and couldn't answer the usual questions satisfactorily. 'The jury returned a verdict in accordance with the facts disclosed.'

Jane, who would become my Great Great Grandma was then fourteen-years old. The unnamed fourteen-month old child who drowned was her little sister Amelia. Jane, Amelia, Mary Ann and the unnamed brother were four of the ten children born to John and Mary Ann Woodall. Jane was the second eldest.

John and Mary Ann married in Adelaide in 1848. John was from Shropshire/Cheshire/Wales depending on what official record you read. Mary Ann was from Cornwall. Her family, Kay, Kane, Cane, Cann, Keam is spelt differently on most records I read.

Jane was born at Pine Hills (presumably Pine Hills Station) near Harrow in Western Victoria in 1850. In 1852, Jane and two of her siblings were baptised at Lake Wallace, the Minister was from the St Stephens Parish in Portland. Her dad is listed as a 'shepherd'. The town of Edenhope was established on the shores of Lake Wallace. This did not occur until 1864.

Mary Ann died in the Ararat Hospital on the 20th July 1870 aged forty-seven years from a malignant disease of the brain.

Three years before her mother's death, at the age of sixteen, Jane married Richard Smart. They lived in the Ararat area raising ten children. Jane died on 15th August 1935. A widow for forty-one years she buried four of her own children before she died.

But who was Jane?

I can trace a line in the dust from Adelaide to Pine Hills to Lake Wallace to Port Curtis (outside Ararat). I'm assuming her father John was chasing gold (Port Curtis was a mining area) and the short stays along the way working or shepherding on the large properties were to fund the trip. Historical records state property owners found it difficult to keep working men or replace those who left chasing gold. On unfenced land as these early properties were, a high labour force was necessary to keep track of stock during the day, erect mobile wooden fencing at night to protect the stock and to ensure all areas of the land were used for grazing to ensure the land regulations were obeyed.

In some respects, I envy my Great, Great Grandma Jane. The first sight her baby eyes saw was the Australian landscape in its virgin state before trees were cleared, before fences and roads divided the vast spaces she travelled with her family. Jane knew no different. Her parents came from other lands, for Jane and her siblings this was the norm, this was home. I wonder how they travelled, what possessions they had, what food they ate? Along the way Jane's mum, Mary Ann, was pregnant and gave birth. How utterly scary would this have been, miles and miles and miles from any form of help, from any woman to ask for advice, to talk to about birthing and feeding, about caring for sick children, about dealing with dirty nappies and all that goes with little children. What shelter did they have? As a shepherd it would have been a very basic hut. On the road from one place to the next there would have been no shelter other than any temporary structures they created themselves. Did they have a wagon and horse? Was it big enough to carry them all? Quite possibly not, even very young children had to walk at times or take turns in the wagon.

I may envy Jane experiencing the Australian landscape in its virgin state, but this really highlights my ignorance of what these families endured. I can read about the Edgar family who settled Pine Hills Station just as I can read about the Hope brothers who settled at Lake Wallace. Baby Jane was part of those histories, but her parents don't rate a mention in the history books. They did not succeed and prosper as did the Edgar family and the Hope brothers. The Edgar and Hope families worked extremely hard in harsh conditions to achieve what they did, but their stories are told in history books. Their achievements live on. Their descendants look back and can see where and who they came from.

Ordinary people are lost between the pages of history books, lost between lines on the pages, sometimes they peep out of local papers, for a brief moment their names are recorded as Jane's was with the sad drowning of her little sister. The paper doesn't record the grief, it is merely a clinical account of an inquest. The reader is left to imagine the sorrow, never forgotten, by parents and siblings. What does it tell me of fourteen-year-old Jane who one day would become my Great, Great Grandma?

Jane was practical and responsible. She went 'to look for my sister, having missed her.' Jane searched, heard Mary Ann calling her, went to her 'and found her with the deceased'. Jane gathered up the limp little girl in her arms and rushed to her brother. Jane then ran to her mother who was visiting a neighbour about half a mile off. Not once in all of these terrible few moments in discovering Amelia had drowned did she collapse in tears and leave someone else to carry out these tasks. Did she cry? Was she sobbing when she saw her mother and had to tell her what had happened? Were the other children crying? Where was the little girl buried? The emotionless wording of the Inquest report gives us only facts. The effect of Amelia's death on the family is not recorded. I read the inquest report in an old newspaper. It has not been passed from generation to generation. As I research Jane's siblings it is interesting to note many of these siblings chose the name Amelia when naming their children.

The obituaries in the Ararat paper when Jane died tell me, 'The Rev. G. Fisher, of the Methodist Church, assisted by the Rev. S. J. Hill, of St. Andrews Presbyterian Church, conducted the services at the house and grave.' Following the service at the house, 'The cortege moved from the residence of her son.' Jane died in the Ararat Hospital, she left for her burial from the residence of her son. The person who wrote up the report of the funeral said, 'a large number of wreaths were placed on the casket, including one from the Royal Black Preceptory, 26 and 27, Ararat.'

This obituary implies Jane was a woman of faith. The fact two Ministers of Religion presided over the services at the house and grave indicates Jane was actively involved in the life of these two Protestant denominations. There is a significance I think, that the journalist considered it important to mention one of the wreaths on the casket was from the Royal Black Preceptory. I have very little knowledge or understanding of the Royal Black Preceptory other than it is a tiered organisation with the local Preceptory known as the Royal Black Preceptory and is the base of the tiers. The foundations of the organisation are firmly based on scriptural truths and following the Christian Reformed Faith. Was Jane a member of this Preceptory or in some way affiliated with them or was the wreath a sign of respect for this woman of faith?

Jane is my Great, Great Grandma. She is my mum's Great Grandma. Mum was about eight when her Great Grandma died but she never mentioned meeting her. Perhaps she didn't. The circumstances of her mother's illness, the fact she lived in Warracknabeal and her parents in Broadford and Great Grandma in Ararat may have made the journey impractical. Mum's maternal grandfather was Jane's son. He died ten years before his mother Jane. Family relationships can become distorted and disconnected for many reasons. Yet, I sense a connection, learnt but not taught.

13. Jane Woodall (Smart)

*

Mum's parents, Bob and Allie, were married in a Presbyterian Church. Mum was baptised in a Presbyterian Church. Allie's parents' funerals were both conducted by Church of England clergy. Allie's paternal grandparents however, Richard and Jane, were married in a Wesleyan Church and both buried by Wesleyan Minsters, with a Presbyterian Minister also assisting at Jane's funeral. Did Allie visit her paternal grandmother when she was young? What relationship did Allie have with her paternal grandmother? Her paternal grandfather died before she was born. What made her and Bob choose a Presbyterian Church for their wedding? I can only make assumptions which may be incorrect, but I wonder what influence Jane may have had in the life of Allie. What did Allie learn from the way her Grandma Jane lived her life?

I feel I do Jane a disservice in knowing so little about her. What I do know, her many years as a widow, the adult children she mourned and buried, the trauma of the drowning of her little sister are all sadness. But the image I have of the essence of Jane, and I don't know where this image of essence comes from, is a woman who found a great sense of fulfilment in the life she led. Perhaps as a woman of faith she found strength from her faith in her times of sadness but a hope in her times when the journey was less rough. Unfortunately the highlights of a person's existence are often the sad or difficult times, the ordinary days are not recorded, the times of laughter, the family celebrations, the events that are not significant but bring pleasure, the friends Jane had and the family who visited. Jane is there somewhere, her individual thread as strong and as vital to the family cloth I'm weaving with words as are the threads of those I am more familiar with.

Top: Yvonne, feeding her Grandma's adult dog, Mick. (about 1935)

Middle: Yvonne, with her maternal Grandma in Broadford feeding a lamb. (about 1935)

Bottom: Yvonne, or Bonny as her family called her, as a baby with her Mum and two of her cousins. (about 1928).

Top: Auntie (Mary Jefferies) with Judith and Michael's two sons, Peter and David. (about 1984)

Middle: Judith with her paternal Grandma feeding one of her Grandpa's lambs, (about 1955)

Right: Alice Clark/Smart with one of her grandchildren. (about 1948)

Top left: Charlotte Chamberlain/Avery.

Top right: Kate Creswick/Jefferies in front of the cottage her husband William built.

Middle: Amy Boon/Hancock with her husband James and their dog, Trip.

Opposite top: St Anne's in Oldland Common, in Bristol where Eliza Hunt and Robert Jefferies married.

Opposite middle: Ann Toop/Boon (seated centre) with some of the four generations of her family. Judith's Dad is the toddler attempting to escape. (about 1928)

Opopsite bottom: Gwennap Church in the village of Gwennap, Cornwall – spiritual home to generations of the Hancock, Bray and Bishop families.

Top: Martha Shackley/Avery and her husband Richard.

Bottom left: Harriet Roberts/Chamberlain. (about 1890)

Bottom right: A portrait created from convict records portraying how Mary Murphy may have looked when she was 16 years old.

Top left: this magnificent Redwood tree in Campbell's Creek Cemetery is directly opposite the Wesleyan section where Thomas Boundy, the second husband of Thomasina Bray/Bishop/Boundy is buried. His unmarked grave is the first grave in the Wesleyan section.

Top right: St Mary the Virgin Church in Compton Pauncefoot, spiritual home to generations of the Foote and Smart families.

Bottom: St George Church in Modbury, where many of the children of Ann Whiteway and John Bickford were baptised.

14
Mary Hughes (Creswick)
1827 – 1890

Spring was nudging winter into hibernation when Mary's daughter Kate gave birth to her firstborn, Robert Leonard, on 15th August 1890. Mary made the trip from St Arnaud to Warracknabeal not only to see her new grandson but to help Kate during those first busy, tiring weeks of motherhood. Soon after Mary's arrival, however, Kate was not only caring for a newborn but caring for her mother who had become seriously ill with pyemia, (blood poisoning). Mary's condition deteriorated. The Parish Priest was called from Horsham to administer the last rites. My Great, Great Grandma Mary may have been dying but her determination was not deteriorating, she desperately wanted to die at home in St Arnaud. A covered cart or wagon was hired. Mary returned to St Arnaud. Today the trip from St Arnaud to Warracknabeal takes a little over an hour. I can only imagine what the trip must have been like for Mary, a dying woman, on the rough dirt roads of the late 1800s. She died in the St Arnaud Hospital on 28th November 1890. Ten weeks later her daughter Kate and her husband William buried their baby son Robert Leonard in the Warracknabeal cemetery. His cause of death was 'Diarrhoea' and Asthenia.

Mary is buried in the St Arnaud cemetery, several short steps from where her husband William was buried in 1885. The physical distance between their final resting places may be short, the religious chasm between them however was immense. William is buried in the Church of England section, Mary in the Roman Catholic section. Mary is buried in the same grave as her daughter-in-law Maggie and her grandson William. Her husband William is buried in the same grave as one of their sons, also a William. I suspect Mary was desperate to return to St Arnaud to be buried in the same cemetery as her husband in the town they had called home since the very early days of their marriage. William was from Sheffield in Yorkshire, Mary from Armagh in County Armagh, they both said goodbye to the places of their birth embracing this land as their new home. In death their religious differences meant they could not be buried together but they could be buried in the same cemetery.

A story handed on from generation to generation is William was disowned for marrying Mary, a poor, Catholic, Irish girl. I'm not sure which was the greatest crime, being poor, Catholic or Irish, perhaps the sum of the three was too great. They married in Benalla on the seventh day of November in 1856. Their first child was born in Geelong, their next ten children in St Arnaud.

The road Mary and William followed is paved with questions. Were they married in the Catholic tradition or the Church of England tradition? How did they meet? When did William arrive in Australia? When did Mary arrive in Australia? What work did each of them do before they chose to chase gold in St Arnaud? For 'miner' was William's occupation noted on the birth record of their second child. He worked the Bell Rock Reef while Mary cared for a toddler and a newborn. Their home was a goldfields tent.

By 1863 William is still a miner but he owns a brick house on the Melbourne Road. During his life in St Arnaud William was a miner, a labourer, a fruiterer and a County Court Bailiff. William, Mary and their children, while growing up, continued to live in a brick house on the same allotment number.

For many years as I travelled from our home to Warracknabeal I entered St Arnaud from the Avoca Road. Then I varied my route on leaving our home, so I no longer had to deal with city or suburban traffic but was always on country roads. It was a pleasure to experience the seasons as I journeyed through the varying countryside. I now entered St Arnaud on the Melbourne Road which is the cemetery side of the town. The first time I gently turned the steering wheel negotiating the final curve before passing the houses on the edge of town I decided I preferred this entrance to St Arnaud. In the years of my many, many trips along this route as Mum and Dad's health deteriorated I always felt a sense of joy not only in the familiarity of the curve, but a sense of belonging. Once through St Arnaud I was on the last stretch to home. Very recently, with the help of a researcher at the St Arnaud Historical Centre I discovered the part of St Arnaud Mary and William called home is very close to the Melbourne Road.

Three stories have woven their way through the generations about Mary. The first concerns her death. The second is William's family disowning him for marrying Mary. The third relates to Mary as a storyteller.

Great, Great Grandma Mary gathered her family around her entertaining them with stories of Ireland. The family wasn't wealthy but always the words 'gathered the family' and 'entertained the family' weave between the names and dates of the children growing and flexing their wings before marrying and creating families of their own. The stories are part of the summer dust and squelched into the winter mud now, but the warmth of being gathered together is not lost. Mary also knew great sorrow. Of the eleven children Mary gave birth to, there were three little Williams and a Mary buried before they'd even reached school age. A sadness I assume Mary carried with her to her own grave. Another daughter had an illegitimate child. I don't know the story of the father, but the child and the single daughter remained in the home until she married a man who became Dad to the child she already had.

On a recent visit to St Arnaud we drove around the town looking at some of the historical buildings, many still in use but for different purposes than originally built for. I reflected on the fact Mary and William would have seen these buildings when being used for their original purpose. Then I realised Mary and William were in St Arnaud *before* these buildings were built. The older of their children would have attended the Bark Hut School not far from their house. This school has long gone, only the general area where it was is known. They were part of a community planning for a future of their town and building buildings that would last. In the grainy old photos when many of the community were present for the laying of foundation stones or other celebrations William, Mary and their children are possibly in these photos. If not in the photos, were part of the community excitement as their town became a place more permanent than the gold field tents.

St Arnaud is dry, dusty and hot in summer. However, in July 1882 it snowed in St Arnaud (as well as in other places in Victoria and NSW not known for snow). I imagine the delight for Mary and William for their children to experience snow where previously, they had only known what snow was from the stories Mary was so fond of telling them. Did she gather her children to her, some now adults, as she excitedly told them of the regular snow she had experienced in Armargh? The cold, the flakes floating in the air, a reminder for many, of the places they had left far beyond the oceans, a new experience for those born in the land of their parents' choice.

I visited Armagh in County Armagh a couple of years ago. As we walked and drove through the undulating, narrow streets I pondered on how Mary learnt to adapt to the flat plains around St Arnaud. We stood on a hill overlooking the town so very different to the small community Mary and William brought their children up in. It must have been overwhelming and challenging, yet illiterate Mary, through her storytelling brought Ireland with her, brought home with her. As she created a new home in St Arnaud, the home of her childhood lived within her and within her children. From the familiarity of their birthplace they were connected to a place none of them would ever see. Whatever Mary had experienced in Ireland, whatever had happened to make her choose to move across the oceans she 'entertained' her family with stories of Ireland connecting family and place.

As we drove through Armagh, down a narrow, narrow street with two-way traffic and cars parked either side of the street we approached a street sign pointing to 'The Shambles'. Aware of the history of streets labelled 'The Shambles' I felt a sudden sense of 'Mary would have walked down here'. The realisation the narrow, narrow street would have been here when Mary lived here caused an unexpected surge of emotion within me. Almost catching a glimpse of a woman hurrying towards The Shambles, her skirt buffeting in the wind I knew the gap between then and now too great to see her face, too great for Mary to know I was looking for her, but I like to think I took her home for a while.

Whenever I go home to Warracknabeal I go through St Arnaud. I often stop at the Queen Mary Gardens for a break. In the difficult years when Mum had dementia the stop was significant. I would take a walk around the gardens – the seasons were visual with the grand oaks, the lush green lawns of winter and spring, the thin dryness of late summer and autumn even with dedicated watering, the nativity display in December. There was a time the nativity display wasn't protected. The characters rearranged by passers-by or young children. Times change, as the saying goes, today the nativity display is protected with wire mesh walls and roof. Baby Jesus was only behind wire mesh for the month of December. How many Decembers have some of the refugees experienced in detention? I don't go to Warracknabeal for Christmas anymore. I'm not sure if the nativity display is still there.

As I walked around the gardens, past the statue of Marshal Jacques Leroy de St Arnaud, towards the fountain in the middle of the ornamental lake it was a physical act of letting go of one place and focusing on where I was going. I couldn't be in two places at once – coming or going I let go of one and embraced the other. I often thought of Mary, keeping alive her Irish home so far away as she created another home in Australia. St Arnaud always felt like another home to me. Perhaps Mary was gathering me in, or perhaps the image of Mary within her family circle reminded me of the times before Mum had dementia.

The plants in the Queen Mary Gardens were in the early stages of growing when William died in 1885. Five years later when the gardens were revealing their true beauty Mary died. At the time of her death Mary was working as a laundress at the local hospital. I'm not sure if it had been a long-time position or if she'd had to go out to work after William died. The youngest child was only nine when William died. After Mary died her daughter Kate gathered him in until he too was ready to find his own way. In six years, Kate lost her dad, she married, had her first child, lost her mother-in-law (who was in a mental asylum) lost her mum and then her baby. Still she gathered in her youngest brother and her father-in-law.

Sometimes, when our family is gathered together, when stories are told, new anecdotes added, stories are repeated, (repeated stories are like Grandma hugs when Grandma is no longer present), I sense a presence, as I used to sense a presence in Auntie's house when we gathered in her kitchen telling stories, as I sensed a presence when I walked around the Queen Mary Gardens, I feel the brush of a skirt beside me, the faintest touch of a hand against mine as Great, Great Grandma Mary gathers us in.

15
Eliza Hunt (Jefferies)
1839 – 1891

Great, Great Grandma Eliza spent the last fourteen years of her life in Aradale in Ararat. It was at the time, known as a lunatic asylum. But her existence is not a weak thread in our family cloth. Sometimes we can't fix things, sometimes we can't make things right, sometimes life isn't fair and sometimes a person's world, like Eliza's, goes so 'pear-shaped' it can't be reshaped. Our resilience is not strengthened in focusing on those who were resilient but to embrace those who were not. In embracing those who were not we take the risk of recognising our own vulnerabilities. However distressing I find Eliza's story I do not have the power to change it, but I do have the power, as we all do, to create that sense of belonging, the sense of inclusion in family or community, amongst my female friends providing support when their world goes 'pear shaped', a safe place when the world is too harsh. Sometimes simply being there for someone walking a similar path is all we can do, and it is enough. Sometimes it isn't enough. We only fail when we turn our back and walk away because we believe the person simply lacks resilience without attempting to understand what it was that weakened their resilience.

15. Eliza Hunt (Jefferies)

St Anne's Church in Oldland didn't have a postal address when we visited so didn't show up on the GPS. It is not a grand cathedral on a hill commanding attention, it is not a church with spires pointing to the heavens sign posting where it is, it is a small, welcoming church – physically and as a faith community – nestled amidst homes. It doesn't even have a car park but can be approached from more than one direction. When we were close to finding it, we didn't know how close until a passer-by pointed it out. We were too late for the service we hoped to attend but not too late to be welcomed by friendly parishioners.

I was disappointed to miss the service but deep within it reflected Great, Great Grandma Eliza and the very slight grasp I have on the thread weaving her story within the family cloth.

Eliza and Robert married at St Anne's in February 1862, a few weeks before they set sail for Australia. One of the pews, reminiscent of a time when a family subscribed or paid for a pew still bears a plaque with Robert's family name.

Eliza and Robert had three children, each born in different rural towns in Victoria. In 1875 Eliza spent three months in what was then called Kew Asylum. She was discharged after this time as she 'was desperate to get home to family'. Records do not record what mental illness she was suffering from to necessitate her admission other than she was suffering from delusions about land and was dangerous. At this time they were living in Purrumbete, near Camperdown, possibly on a small block of land Robert had selected. By 1877 when Eliza was admitted to Aradale they were living on selected land in an area we now know as Birchip, true Mallee country. The family story is Robert's land was now where the township of Birchip is situated. About 1920, when one of Eliza and Robert's grandsons was working in a Bank in Birchip 'Jefferies Hut' was still standing.

Eliza and Robert's tenure of their selection was short-lived. Rabbits ate their hopes and dreams. In May 1877, Robert took Eliza to the Police Station in Donald and had her committed to a lunatic asylum. It was an era when a mental illness was treated differently to a physical illness, as though mental illness was a crime. Records state, 'Robert was in very straitened circumstances and could not afford anyone to look after her'. They were almost starving poor. The same records state Eliza was constantly roaming, 'looking for their grand estates.'

Eliza died in the lunatic asylum almost fourteen years later. Aradale, which is where Eliza spent those fourteen years is no longer operational as a mental health facility. Parts of it are now used by Melbourne Polytechnic for its wine making course. The old buildings are open for tour groups at set times. I was surprised at the beauty of the architecture. Surprised to learn so much of what was used to build the buildings in the 1860s was made in Australia. I wasn't surprised to learn Ararat and Beechworth were chosen as sites for mental health facilities because of their distance from Melbourne and in isolated areas where they were away from the sight of the general public. I'm not sure if the massive wall surrounding the whole site was to keep those committed safe from the public or to keep the public safe from those committed. Over the many decades of its use until 1998 the facility housed those suffering from an immense variety of mental illnesses; there was a 'retard' wing (I say the word with great distaste and refuse to start it with an upper-case 'r', but the word reflects an era). 'retard' covers not only those who may have been born with an intellectual disability but those who were unable to learn to read and write. Today, some of these people would be called dyslexic. It was an era we would rather ignore or find extremely offensive. But ignore it we must not.

It is rare to find huge amounts of records for the 100 plus years Aradale was functioning. For the facilities such as Aradale and Beechworth were places where people were placed and forgotten about. Not only the committed, but those who were employed to care for the patients are forgotten as well. We were lucky to find a few records about our Eliza. We were lucky Eliza's husband, children and grandchildren did not forget about Eliza. Her story, the little we know, has passed from one generation to another. Not only Eliza's story but Robert's story, for he did not commit Eliza to get rid of her, but he was so poor he could not afford anyone to care for her. The only family they had remained in England, their children too young to be able to care for their mother as their father attempted to scratch a living from a dusty earth. He was never the same again, so the family story goes. He never came to terms with having to commit his wife to a lunatic asylum. If the family couldn't care for her, they were not ashamed of her, not ashamed of her story, she is as much a part of the family as are those who lived their lives freely beyond the asylum walls.

15 . Eliza Hunt (Jefferies)

I lose the family for some years after Robert has Eliza committed. Lose the road they followed. Ada the first born died at the age of 21 in Donald. I'm not sure where Robert was working and living then or where the other two children were. In 1889 Robert's son William married a St Arnaud girl, Kate. They moved to Warracknabeal into the two-bedroomed weatherboard cottage William had already built. Robert too, moved to Warracknabeal and either lived with them or close by and worked at one of the local hotels as a gardener. Eliza died in 1891. I suspect she was dead and buried before the news reached Robert she had died. Eliza was one of the lucky ones. Her records record her husband's name. As a family we can find her in government records, find her death registered with the name of her husband, the man who never got over committing her, recorded in that final document proving her existence. She is buried in a common grave in the Ararat cemetery with four other people.

About 1900 Robert moved to Western Australia to live with his daughter, Amelia, his son-in-law Thomas and their children. Amelia died in 1910. Robert in 1911. When he moved to Western Australia, he left behind his marriage certificate tucked safely into the Bible presented to Eliza in 1861. They are the only things we have touched by Eliza. The Bible is now in my care.

I'll never know what mental illness Eliza suffered from. The autopsy report after her death said her 'bowels were gelatinous'. If the information I gained from googling 'gelatinous bowels' can be trusted there is the possibility she suffered from a bowel condition which if left untreated can cause mental disorder. We know this today. I'm not sure it even had a name in the mid 1800s and if it did poor people had little opportunity to access such information.

Eliza may have had manic depression, a common disorder amongst migrants, one of the common disorders for those committed to the lunatic asylums. The chasm between the home they had come from to their life in Australia too great to cross. The landscape so vastly different to what their eyes were accustomed to, the sounds of the bush or the unmade streets of the larger towns did not match the sounds of home, wherever they turned the people they met were not the ones they left behind. For many, the reality and the dream did not become one. It was all too hard. Was that why Eliza took to wandering, searching for their vast estates in a land fast becoming a dust bowl as Robert and other selectors cleared a land held together by the trees they were tearing down and populated by rabbits eating the little they could grow?

A couple of years ago I bought a book titled *The Long Gaze Back*. It is an anthology of Irish Women Writers. As I read one of the short stories *Three stories about love* by Anne Enright my mind suddenly thought of Eliza. The character in the story is a young pregnant Irish woman living in Australia. 'She missed her mother. Really missed her. And it was a very big planet.' Soon after awakening one morning she says to her husband, 'You're not far away until you have a baby, and then you're really, really far away.' Was that Eliza's problem? Did she feel she was no longer living in the shelter of one another and it all became too hard?

I hope the fact her children, her children's children and then their children still respect her story, keep her name in place in the family story and treasure their family relationships will give Eliza some peace and cease her endless search for 'grand estates'. 'Grand estates' are sometimes mansions on rich, fertile land. Other times they are the richness of living in the shelter of one another. None of us have mansions on rich, fertile land but I'd like to tell Eliza we are rich in the shelter of one another. It is her story which reminds each of us not to take this precious gem for granted.

Dear Mum,

In your dementia years you often talked of Eliza. I sometimes tried to guide the conversation along a different path, but you would ignore my efforts. 'I wonder how Eliza felt,' you'd say, 'when Robert left her?' Other times, 'I wonder how Eliza felt when the family never came to see her.' Sometimes you'd talk of our visit to Aradale. 'The buildings were different to what I expected,' you would comment, 'they were quite splendid, weren't they?' I could agree with you on that. 'Perhaps Eliza felt she had found her grand estates,' I'd respond. You always smiled then, as if in agreement. Other times, 'Poor Eliza, being left there. I wonder if she understood?'

I'm not sure I tried to guide the conversation along a different path for your benefit or for mine. Despite the splendid architecture and the beauty of the structures, the silence of the empty buildings held no peace for me. The steps leading to one of the sections Eliza would have worked in are hollowed in the centre so many feet have walked up and down them. How often did Eliza walk those steps searching not only for their grand estates but the family she was so desperate to get home to?

I know in your dementia years you felt we had failed you Mum. As the layers of your living peeled away you recalled your mum being cared for by your maternal Grandmother, your Grandmother caring for her husband and your mother's siblings until their deaths. You talked of Auntie caring for her father at home until his death, how he was laid out at home. How she cared for her mother at home until the last few days of her life. Our decision for you to go into residential care was in your eyes an act of abandonment. As you attempted to make sense of your dementia framed world you identified with Eliza. The circumstances were vastly different but somehow in identifying with Eliza you seemed to understand how Eliza may have felt in a way I could not for I was identifying with Robert knowing he was making the best, the only decision he could make in the circumstances. Making the right decision, Mum, knowing the person you are deciding for will be unhappy leaves a sense of disquiet that never goes away. It just never goes away, Mum.

Love,

Judith

16
Ann Toop (Boon)
1840 - 1934

Great, Great Grandma Ann was born within sight of Stonehenge as she frequently told anyone who would listen. Her often-repeated stories of the ancient rocks of Wiltshire were synonymous with eye-rolling and barely-suppressed sighs from family members.

As the Boangeres rode the swell in 1862 and the coastline of England faded Ann knew she would never see Stonehenge again, neither would she walk the familiar streets of Dilton Marsh, the village of her birth, again. As night settled like a shroud around the ship, Ann felt as though she was an insignificant dot on an ocean as vast and as unknown as her future was. Her thoughts rocked with the rhythm of the boat oscillating between her sister Eliza's growing family in Clunes and the ancient rocks of Stonehenge anchored to the earth, unchanging and immoveable. Whatever challenges this new adventure may bring Stonehenge would not change. It was her rock in an unknown tomorrow.

I've been to Stonehenge, seen the countryside around Ann's birthplace of Dilton Marsh. The green of English landscapes creeps to the edge of the bitumen, a soft, soothing green nourished in a consistent rainfall. Home for me is not such a green. Even in a bumper season when the rainfall comes at the right time, the crops flourish and the roadside verges are overtaken with green it isn't an English green. Our visit to England could be counted in weeks. We were too busy exploring to be homesick but sometimes as we drove through the lush green fields I looked forward to when the English green was a memory and we were driving through the dusty, open paddocks of the landscapes I know.

Dilton Marsh, the village of Ann's birth, is on a hill. The day we visited it was cloudy and hazy. We could not see the edge of town let alone the eighteen road miles to Stonehenge. Could Ann actually see Stonehenge from Dilton Marsh? It was disappointing to not be able to prove or disprove the story, but in reality it was proven. Whether Ann could physically see it or not, she knew it was in her home territory.

Dad knew his Great Grandma Ann. 'She always seemed an old lady to me,' he said. Dad was nearly seven when Ann died in 1934, aged ninety-three. The significance of Dad's story was his impression was created not with a single visit but many visits. Ann was cared for by family until her death, those who had moved to other areas came home regularly to visit. Ann's voice may have been silenced with her death but the story of Ann's connection to Stonehenge lives on.

Ann, the daughter of a weaver who had died very young was brought up by her mother as were her siblings. As a single parent those years would have been very challenging for Ann's mum. It is interesting to note that Ann could read and write, signing her marriage certificate with a neat clear hand.

Ann's sister, Eliza, sailed for Australia in 1859 marrying Phillip Parsons soon after arrival. I'm assuming Eliza already knew Phillip, perhaps he had been a neighbour, one of the Parsons from Dilton Marsh or perhaps she met him while in service in London. Phillip had a seafaring background but took up gold mining in Clunes. Maybe the two sisters planned for Ann to migrate before Eliza had left England. On the Boangeres' records Ann is listed as 'Servant'. On her marriage certificate in the profession or trade column 'none' is listed. For many young women, as independent as many of them were in migrating to Australia alone, it was in the early years of motherhood they felt the chasm between Australia and the country of their birth. As childbirth approached, and the responsibility of caring for young children became a reality, these women yearned to be closer to their mothers and female siblings for support. This may have been Ann's role once she arrived in Australia.

In 1864, in the home of her sister and brother-in-law, both of them official witnesses, Ann married James Bickford Boon according to the rites of the Wesleyan church. Like her brother-in-law, Ann's husband had a seafaring background having served an apprenticeship with the British Navy as a ship's carpenter. The family story goes he was lured by the prospect of discovering gold. He may have worked in one of the mines for a very brief period of time but soon took up his trade as a carpenter. In a gold mining town where shopkeepers and miners were keen to fold away their canvas tents to work or live in more weather-proof dwellings a carpenter could earn gold with more certainty than miners digging in the ground. The two couples followed the same faith path. As Ann and James started their own family the two sisters supported one another. Ann and James' children born in Clunes were baptised into the Wesleyan faith. At least two of their children were baptised by James' Uncle, his mother's brother, Rev. James Bickford.

While family was obviously important to Ann and James, they made other friends within the Methodist or Wesleyan community – particularly Lavinia and Richard Hancock. In the mid-1870s the Boon and Hancock families selected land at Avon Plains sharing their next adventure. Ann's sister Eliza and her husband Phillip remained in Clunes on their own land.

In searching for gold, the miners dug deep wounds into the earth. As farmers, which they became in the move to Avon Plains, they nurtured the earth to grow crops and feed their animals. The land was new to such cultivation. The indigenous people had nurtured the land for thousands of years but the expansion of the migrants beyond the coastal regions of Australia dug deep wounds into the lives of the indigenous people forcing them from their traditional lands. Generally, our history books give a brief first chapter to the 'first people' of Australia and a rich many chapters to the first settlers. I cannot change what my ancestors have done but as I research their lives, telling their stories, I sense an uncomfortable silence in the untold stories of the land before their arrival.

Ann and James named their property at Avon Plains 'Modbury' after James' birthplace in Devon.

16. Ann Toop (Boon)

New land, fencing, becoming farmers, building a home, building a community with other landowners, life at Avon Plains with young families to rear would have been exciting, challenging and at times quite scary. In the early days of settlements in Australia, faith communities were central to the development of the community in general. Ann's husband James, previously a ship's carpenter, had welcome skills when it came to building the Methodist Church at Avon Plains. Experienced with climbing heights to build ships he had no problems building the roof of the church.

It was in this Church in September 1887, Amy, the daughter of Ann and James Boon married James, son of Lavinia and Richard Hancock. They commenced their married life farming at Avon Plains and their first child, Alice, (my paternal grandma) was born there. She was baptised in the Church built on land donated by her paternal grandfather, Richard Hancock, beneath the roof of the Church erected by her maternal grandfather, James Boon.

In the July 21, 1916 issue of the Spectator and Methodist Chronicle an article was published titled 'The Cities of the Plains'. The area being discussed was as broad as Kyabram, Shepparton, Horsham, Donald and Warracknabeal. The writer was urging the reader to consider a life beyond the city boundaries. Many names are listed of staunch Methodist families who had contributed to the faith communities within these areas. The Boon and Hancock names are amongst those listed.

As family stories and generations weave in and out I'm reminded of Ann's dad, the weaver, Jeremiah. Sharing the journey on the *Boangeres* with Ann were my great, great grandparents Eliza and Robert Jefferies. There is a strong possibility at some stage during the lengthy voyage Ann, Eliza and Robert conversed. There was no further contact once the ship reached its destination. Their journeys followed different paths, their children flexed their wings choosing their own paths and in time the roads intersected. Robert and Eliza's son chose Warracknabeal as his home as did one of the sons of Ann and James. On the 10th February 1951 the great grandson of Ann and James married the great granddaughter of Eliza and Robert in Warracknabeal. The only link between the two is the ship *Boangeres* but I ponder not only the interconnectedness of journeys, people and place, but how my sense of belonging to place is greater than being born there when those I am descended from on two sides chose to call it home.

I have my birthplace in rural Victoria. When I travel to Warracknabeal there is a long stretch of road once I've passed through St Arnaud when I sense, 'I'm nearly home'. The sky is the blue of home, the countryside familiar, the haze distorting the trees familiar; the seasons of the land are the seasons of my growing up. The wheels of the car hum, 'I'm nearly home, I'm nearly home'. But I have another home, the one my husband and I created for our two sons. When I drive back from Warracknabeal and see the first lights of Melbourne in the distance I sense, 'I'm nearly home'. For me, the plains of Warracknabeal own me as the land of Wiltshire owned Great Great Grandma Ann. But the home I share with my husband is not in second place as I'm sure Avon Plains was not second place for Ann. We cannot be in two places at once but leaving one place does not mean it leaves us.

When I first heard the story of Ann's constant reminder to others of Stonehenge, I wondered why the memory didn't lessen as her time of living in Australia increased. She had after all married and raised a family in Australia. She only lived in Wiltshire for twenty-one years but in Australia for over seventy. However, home is such an integral part of who we are there is an intense desire to keep each home alive within us. I understand Great Great Grandma Ann.

Yet, I know very little about Ann. I can trace her steps in Australia, her marriage, her children, who her children married, who their children were, the children's children and somewhere in that extended family of Ann and James my name is included along with my husband's and our children and their children.

Yet, when I peel away some of the layers of time, I discover snippets of Ann's life when she must have trembled, when she needed the support of those around her. Ann was only three when her Dad died. She was raised by a single mum until her mum remarried when she was fourteen years old. She travelled to Australia alone as a single woman. She married and had children moving to an area with undeveloped land. Her husband died on 2nd February 1906. An infant grandson died on 12th February 1906, buried in the same plot as James. Her sister Eliza died in 1906. At least three of her adult grandsons died in WWI. One of her daughters died in 1922. Through all of this Ann was part of an extended family, part of a community she had helped to create, part of a faith community as were her children. Through all of this Ann clung to Stonehenge, those ancient, mysterious rocks placed in a formation historians are still attempting to explain. When her new world was overwhelming, when life went 'belly-up', Ann maintained her connection with her beginnings. Stonehenge was beyond her line of vision, but she knew it would never change. In telling her story she connected her world with those of the generations who would come after her.

As I stood contemplating Stonehenge I thought of Ann, of my dad as a little boy holding the hand of an old lady he never forgot, an old lady who as a little girl touched the ancient rocks of Stonehenge.

17
Lavinia Bishop (Hancock)
1831 - 1919

Granite and rusted ironwork surround a double plot, the final resting place of Lavinia and Richard Hancock. A rather splendid memorial stone, though moss is now eroding its surface, bears their names, ages and death dates. As I stand in the Methodist section of the Maryborough Cemetery it isn't Lavinia and Richard's deaths, I reflect on but their journey from their Cornish birthplace to this central Victorian country town.

When I attend a burial, my focus is on the person who has recently died, my grief still raw. Yet, when I stand before graves of my forebears as I am on this day, I sense a bigger picture, not of their deaths but their life journey. It's winter, the day is cold and bleak. I'm the only visitor in this silent place. From a distant corner I hear the faint roar of a ride-on mower. It is too far away to smell the newly cut grass mingling with the tang of petrol. As I walk along the path separating the Methodist and Church of England sections, I pass equipment ready to fill some holes in the single-car-only pathway. The workman gives me a silent nod and a whisper of a smile.

Lavinia and Richard were both miners. Every day men, women and children descended shafts into tin and copper mines working in wet, foul-aired conditions to earn a living. Gwennap may have been in one of the richest tin and copper areas in the world but this did not reflect in the pay and conditions of those who worked deep beneath the earth.

On the 19th April 1851 the two twenty-year-olds, Lavinia and Richard, married in the Gwennap Church in Cornwall. Nine days later they set sail from Plymouth on the *Omega*. It arrived in South Australia on the 30th July 1851. According to a family story, three of Richard's brothers travelled on the same ship with them. From my research, three of Richard's brothers did come to Australia over the following years, just not on the same ship. On the passenger list of the *Omega*, Richard is listed as a miner. Lavinia, now a wife, has no occupation beside her name.

Lavinia and Richard's first child, a son they named Richard, was born in Adelaide in August 1852. I suspect they may have been on the Adelaide goldfields, but I have no proof of this. Thirteen months after their son Richard was born he was baptised in Christ Church in Castlemaine. At that time Christ Church was an old storehouse, a vastly different place of worship to the centuries old Church at Gwennap where Lavinia and Richard married.

As the wind attempts to pluck my scarf from around my neck, I ponder on the five to six-week journey from Adelaide to the Victorian gold fields. When gold was first discovered in Victoria there was no direct route from the central Victorian goldfields to Adelaide where, I have been told, the rate for gold was a better rate than in Melbourne. Wagons laden with gold created a white man's road. There would have been many paths familiar to the indigenous people through these areas, but their gentle footsteps left a path with signposts only they understood. Wagon after wagon churned up the dust or gouged the earth when it rained. Those keen to try their luck, like Lavinia and Richard, followed this road from Adelaide to central Victoria.

Some walked, carrying their few possessions on their back. I'm assuming Lavinia and Richard with a young son to care for had a wagon or dray. They possibly travelled with others, there is a safety in numbers when travelling across an unknown land. Women and children were usually given the more luxurious accommodation of sleeping beneath the wagons at night. Lavinia had been a miner. I can't imagine her sitting day after day in the wagon. I can see her walking beside Richard, as they now rest side by side, as they stood side by side at the rail of the *Omega* as it left the Plymouth port. Horses pulling wagons travel at a slow pace. For Lavinia and Richard, the journey from Adelaide to the central Victorian goldfields was an opportunity to consider future farmland should their luck in the gold mines create the financial resources needed. Lavinia and Richard were seeing this vast, unfenced and uninhabited land with their Cornish eyes for the first time. Yet, they carried images of their birthplace beside these new images. For baby Richard, young as he was, these new images were all he knew. I think of this journey as arduous, it wouldn't have been easy, but I wonder if Lavinia and Richard were filled with anticipation of what their chosen land had to offer and any difficulties were part of the journey.

Lavinia and Richard were residents of the 'pop-up' tent communities on the gold fields, Forest Creek (now Chewton), Amherst and Campbells Creek are places entwined with Lavinia and Richard's names. Constant moving with young babies and frequent pregnancies, living in tents or hastily erected huts was hardly ideal but I sense a community as women supported one another through childbirth and the usual ailments afflicting young children more precariously in the goldfields lifestyle, often resulting in death. Was Lavinia with her strong Christian faith one of those reaching out to those in need?

In 1855 Lavinia received a letter from Cornwall informing her of her dad's death in a mine accident. Another letter months later informed her of her mother's remarriage and the fact her mother (Thomasina) and her new husband, Thomas, along with Thomasina's youngest and Thomas' youngest were emigrating to Australia. They followed the now well-defined track created by the gold wagons to join Lavinia and Richard. I can only imagine the delight and joy when mother and daughter saw one another once again. There were many reunions in those early years as siblings of both Lavinia and Richard migrated to Australia as did siblings of Lavinia's parents.

As communities developed Lavinia and Richard were active participants in such communities. Churches were central to the lives of the people of these communities. In Cornwall both their families had been inspired by John Wesley, the father of Methodism. In each of the fledgling areas they called home they had a strong commitment in building places of worship and faith communities around the non-conformist denomination of Methodist they had been exposed to since their early childhood days.

It is believed a depression in the ground called the 'Gwennap Pit' was created when the surface of the earth collapsed into an abandoned mine. John Wesley preached in the 'Gwennap Pit' for the first time on September 6th, 1762. He preached there another seventeen times over the following years. John Wesley described the pit as being 50 feet deep and 200-300 feet across. It is claimed up to 2000 people could be seated on the sides. A further claim is in 1773 John Wesley preached to his largest congregation ever of supposedly 32,000 at Gwennap Pit! The Pit is still in use today by the Methodist Church for worship services on summer Sunday afternoons. Between 1803 and 1806 miners cut twelve circular terraces forming seats. To be born into a community where the stories of John Wesley's preaching would still be told possibly explains Lavinia and Richard's affiliation with Methodism. It could well be their grandfathers were part of the group of miners who cut the seats.

About 1860 Lavinia and Richard with now four children moved to Clunes, another gold mining area in Victoria. In the 1860s 69% of Clunes' population was Cornish.

It was in Clunes where Lavinia and Richard's plans took another direction when Richard started farming. Mining was an opportunity to save the necessary money to buy their own land and plan for future farming ventures, not only to support their growing family but create farming possibilities for their sons. In the mid-1870s they moved with other families from the Clunes goldfields to Avon Plains outside Donald. What attracted these families to make the move together I cannot be sure of but they shared a strong affiliation with the Methodist denomination assisting in the building of a Church at Avon Plains. They became farmers on undeveloped land requiring clearing before planting crops and acquiring livestock. For Lavinia, with a rapidly growing family the move to Avon Plains was another step of their journey within Australia. Yet they journeyed with others who had left family far beyond the oceans surrounding Australia. Together, the women who moved with their husbands to this unsettled land outside Donald created a community not only for themselves but also other women who moved into the area.

Very often the women of these settlers are the unseen force in creating community. Their husbands are often listed on land titles, on documents when new buildings are built as Richard's was in relation to the church. But it is the women who see the need for schools to educate their children, for hospitals to support them in childbirth and when their families are ill or injured, for places to bury their dead. Very often a cemetery is the first community place needed with a young child to be buried or a fatally injured adult interred. Lavinia was a wife and a mother; official records prove this. I have no other stories, passed from one generation to another to add flesh to the bones of officialdom.

The cold is seeping through the soles of my shoes. My legs are chilled but in this silent place I think of the women who moved here before this cemetery became what it is.

A website 'The Cornishmen of Clunes' has a lengthy list of Cornish men and women who lived in Clunes between 1835–1900. I'm not sure if it is the dedicated research done by the person who set up this website or if it is indicative of the Cornish people but the names of husband and wife and often the maiden name of the wife are given. What a welcome change to read Lavinia's name beside Richard's, Ann's name beside James' and her sister Eliza's name beside Phillip's. There are other Hancock names too, demonstrating the bond between family members as they travelled the gold fields.

Richard and Lavinia moved to Maryborough possibly in retirement. One of their sons, James, married Amy, the daughter of one of their fellow travellers from Clunes to Avon Plains. It is interesting to note at least two of James and Amy's children were born in Maryborough. Family ties were so important in isolated areas with women often travelling to older family members to give birth. Richard established a family company in relation to their farming pursuits but financially supported his sons when they wished to flex their wings and move elsewhere. Lavinia and Richard had taken risks in moving from Cornwall to Australia, Richard probably understood why his own sons wanted to take their own risks. They may have spread their wings, but the family contact remained.

While women were often the unseen or unrecognised force in creating communities within their chosen land, I do not feel these women lacked input in either the choice to migrate or where they lived once they arrived in Australia. Cornwall is a beautiful place, rugged coastline and hilly terrain; villages rich with history of individual families and community stories. Gwennap is a delightful little village with a small church always open for passersby such as ourselves to call in and sit within this place of worship, its history dating further back than 1788 when white people claimed the land of the indigenous people in Australia.

Gwennap's history is embedded in Cornwall's mining history. In the nineteenth century it was considered to be part of the richest square mile in the world. Tin and copper were dug from its soil. But such mining came at immense cost to the health of the miners (many died an early death from lung related diseases), neither did it necessarily equate to the wages miners received. For families to survive, men, women and children descended into the mines. What I saw, as a tourist, was rugged beauty. The ruggedness in digging copper and tin mines was back-breaking hard labour. Men may have dreamed of a better life in another land. Women dreamed the same dream not only for themselves and their miner husbands but for their children to live a life above the earth without their young lungs being tainted by what they breathed at the bottom of the mines. I cannot know what dreams Lavinia and Richard dreamt, what they talked about as they planned their migration or on the sea voyage.

On board the *Omega* with Lavinia and Richard were Jane and Thomas Laurence. On the three-and-a-half-month voyage I assume there would have been conversations between the two couples, but they did not maintain contact after the ship docked. Jane was a sister to Harriet who would become my great, great grandma. One of Harriet's daughters would make the journey from South Australia to Dimboola with her husband and family. One of her grandsons would buy a farm in Warracknabeal and marry one of the granddaughters of Lavinia and Richard whose son had bought a farm in Warracknabeal.

Lavinia was eighty-eight when she died and Richard seventy-seven. You cannot leave the place of your birth and not mourn your leaving, you cannot say farewell to family and not mourn the fact you will never see them again, but Lavinia and Richard, though saddened in leaving Cornwall, lived lives rich in family and community in the land of their choice.

Inherited Touch

I'm shivering now as the cold wind swirls around me. Yet I'm surrounded by family, by names of people I never met who lived long before I was born, but I can trace them on the family tree. They are buried in this place, the community gathering of the dead is one way of thinking of a cemetery. Great Great Grandma Lavinia lived a life far removed from the one I am living and died nine years before my dad was born. But as the chill settles deep within, the distant roar of the ride-on mower now silenced in the completion of its task and the last hole in the pathway is filled I have a sudden sense my paternal grandma once stood where I now stand. For Lavinia and Richard were her grandparents. Grandma was nineteen when her Grandpa Richard died. Thirty-one when her Grandma Lavinia died. She mourned them in their deaths and visited their graves on frequent visits to Maryborough. Lavinia was a widow for twelve years. She too would have stood where I am standing before her husband's grave. Time and death may separate us, but the touch of my grandma's hand bridges the gap.

18
Harriet Roberts (Chamberlain)
1830 - 1890

Great, Great Grandma Harriet is a shadowy figure with a name, an approximate birth date and documented marriage and death dates. She is the lady in a formal photo in a fashionable dress of the era, the wife of William, mother of Charlotte, Martha and Henry, sister to Jane and sister-in-law to Thomas Lawrence.

'I'm not sure when Jane and Thomas came to Australia,' my dad used to say. 'But it was a few years before William. He came out on the same ship as his brother, his brother's wife and their little girl.' The story makes sense. 'William was only nineteen, so he got himself established before Harriet came out. They got married in Australia.' It was the story my dad's dad had told him.

My paternal grandpa (a grandson of Harriet and William) was named Hubert Lawrence. My dad insisted Lawrence was supposed to be spelt Laurence, which was, once again, what his dad told him. 'Probably after Harriet's sister Jane as she helped Harriet with the children a lot. Jane was twelve years older than Harriet.' The story was becoming punctuated with spaces, but dad couldn't fill in the gaps for me.

'All the children were born in Balhannah then they selected land at Wirrabara probably about 1870. They built a wattle and daub hut, which is where Charlotte got married on Christmas Day in 1873. The minister had to ride twenty-five miles on horseback from Melrose for the wedding.' This story has fewer gaps as the marriage certificate for Charlotte and her husband William states they married 'at the residence of the bride's father'. The wattle and daub hut we discovered in recent years had several rooms and a tiled floor. 'Before the Methodist Church was built in Wirrabara the services used to be held in Harriet and William's house.' Dad finished his story.

Harriet, like so many of these women, lived in the shadow of her husband when it comes to records of what community activities women were involved in during the early days of white settlement in Australia. I'm assuming Harriet supported her husband in his community activities. Church services in the beginning were in their home, she would have been aware of the needs of women and children in relation to schools, medical care with the sicknesses prevalent in young children and women having babies. Harriet had been fortunate to have her sister Jane to support her, not all women were so lucky.

Clearing land is hard, back-breaking work generally done by the men, but women were actively involved in farm work. There were animals to care for, cows to milk, sheep to protect, chooks to care for, milk to separate and butter to make from the cream, meals to cook, meat to salt, soap to make, candles to make, clothes to mend and make (by hand), produce to grow to add to family supplies and stores to keep in order and ration – there was no nearby supermarket to dash off to when something ran out. By the time Harriet and William moved to Wirrabara their children were no longer little and were able to be of assistance. It would have still been a tough existence though.

About 1890 Harriet and William built a new home on Chamberlain's Hill, which is still called Chamberlain's Hill today. William had added to his original purchase of land in Wirrabara. The home had twelve-foot ceilings with a different pressed metal ceiling in each room and an eight-foot-wide passage down the centre of the house with five bedrooms off the passage. William and Harriet had been financially successful in their time in Australia.

William was a Trustee when the Wirrabara cemetery was established. He obviously purchased a large plot at some stage, large enough to accommodate at least three bodies side-by-side. The first person interred was Harriet's sister, Jane. She died in January 1882. Where is Jane's husband, Thomas? Harriet died in 1900 and is buried beside her sister. Gravestones stand behind each. There is a space presumably for William. Unfortunately, William died in Glasgow in 1902. He took a trip back to England to see his brothers in Ramsbury in Wiltshire. While there he took a holiday up to Glasgow and was found dead in his hotel room one morning. Accidental death was the Coroner's verdict. The coal heater was turned on full, but the flame had blown out. Accidental death seemed the obvious verdict. The fact the only item found in William's pockets was his steamer return ticket to Australia – all his money was gone – muddies the water somewhat. Murder and theft, the family claim. We'll never know the truth.

The trouble with family stories is someone ponders on possibilities which make sense, to fill in the gaps in the stories. In the course of time the possibilities are passed on as fact. The family researcher needs to source original documentation to discover not only the facts but how the stories can warp descendants' impressions of those who lived before them.

Jane and Thomas Lawrence actually arrived in South Australia in 1851, the same year as William, although they sailed on different ships. William travelled with his brother, his brother's wife and their little girl. Shipping records give their names and arrival dates, the 1851 Census in England, which was taken before their departure, sets them in a place. William was born in Ramsbury in Wiltshire County and was a farm labourer before emigrating. Jane and Thomas were not born in Ramsbury but married there in 1840. Thomas was a farm labourer in Ramsbury at the time of the Census.

On arrival in Adelaide, Jane and Thomas, along with William, settled in Balhannah in the Adelaide hills. The two agricultural labourers, who possibly dreamed of owning their own land, at some stage pooled their financial resources, buying land together. How often did these two men and Jane discuss migrating to Australia? Their plans were made before they stepped on board their ships.

The essence of the stories Dad had passed on to me are true but the facts I am discovering to fill in the gaps create a far richer story of the relationship between Jane and Thomas, Harriet and William. With William and Thomas owning some land together and obviously working together it is obvious the story of Jane helping Harriet with the children when they lived so close is true.

Thomas died in September 1881. He and Jane had stayed in Balhannah when Harriet and William moved to Wirrabara. I'm not sure what Thomas died of, but it was William who was responsible for his estate and he and Harriet took Jane into their own home in Wirrabara. Jane died four months later. Harriet mourned the passing of a sister. William mourned the passing of close friends.

An ad in an Adelaide paper for the sale of some of the land William and Thomas jointly owned offers the tantalising spelling of Thomas' family as Laurence.

The facts I discover about Harriet change my perception of this previously shadowy figure. She was born in June 1830 (baptised on 4th June) to Stephen and Mary Roberts. She had a brother, William, who was a toddler when she was born. She had two much older sisters, Jane twelve years older and another who was already married with children of her own. There had been other siblings who sadly had died very young. Two months after Harriet was born her mother died. I'm assuming Jane became the carer of baby Harriet and toddler William.

In the 1841 English Census, Harriet is living in Hilcott, North Newnton with her father Stephen and brother William. Neither Harriet nor her brother William can be found in the 1851 Census although her father Stephen is. William sailed on the *Midlothian* in 1848 emigrating to NSW. Where is Harriet? In her death notice in a South Australian paper in 1900 it states she was 'an old colonist of 51 years'. This suggests she arrived in Australia about 1849. The story about her and husband William is on shaky ground. Had they even met before migrating? I cannot find a record of Harriet's arrival in Australia. Quite possibly she was in domestic service. Did she meet up with her brother? Chances are she joined her sister at some stage as Harriet and William marry in Adelaide in 1854.

The fact Harriet obviously migrated as a single nineteen-year-old has changed my perception of her. She left England not to be greeted by a husband-to-be with her life mapped out as a married woman but as a single woman alone.

As I searched for further information, I found Jane and Thomas' marriage certificate. Both their dads were shepherds and Thomas' family name, as is his father's, was spelt Laurence. Harriet and Jane, like their husbands, had to adapt to a vastly different rural environment in Australia but they both came from families who worked the land.

To Harriet, Jane would have been a surrogate Mum. To Harriet's children, Jane would have been more than Aunt Jane, she would have been a surrogate Grandma. Rather like Auntie who cared for my mum was like a grandma to my brother and me.

I now understand why Charlotte and her husband William named my grandpa, Hubert Lawrence/Laurence. It wasn't out of respect for Jane and Thomas or the fact they had no children of their own. But Jane and Thomas were an intangible part of Charlotte's growing up; the 'living in the shelter of one another' she had experienced with no grandparents in Australia.

Harriet's daughter, Charlotte, was known as a formidable woman. From the two photos I have there appears to be little physical resemblance between Harriet and Charlotte and there is no reason why a daughter has to have the same personality as her mother. But, I wonder, did Charlotte inherit or learn her formidableness from her mother or perhaps it was from her Aunt Jane, or maybe both.

19
Martha Shackley (Avery)
1824 - 1896

When Great, Great Grandma Martha died in 1896 the obituary notice in the South Australian Register following her funeral, opened with the following sentence: 'Another old colonist has passed away in the person of Mrs Richard Avery, sen., who died at her residence Pitchgreen Farm, near Woodside, on Sunday, January 19, at the age of seventy-two years.'

Martha and Richard settled on land just outside Woodside in the Adelaide hills soon after the birth of their first child. As Richard ploughed his land he did, on occasions, witness Aboriginal corroborees. By the time Martha and Richard were buried in the grounds of the Inverbrackie Presbyterian Church close to their home, I doubt very few of the descendants of the Aboriginal men Richard witnessed performing the corroborees were still living in the area and able to tell their story of watching a white man plough their land. Martha and Richard named their farm 'Pitchgreen Farm' after the farm of the same name in Bledlow, Buckinghamshire.

But who was Mrs Richard Avery?

19. Martha Shackley (Avery)

Martha was born in 1824 in Buckinghamshire, England, the same county as her husband Richard. She became Mrs Richard Avery on 11th November 1846. Soon after their marriage they sailed from Plymouth, on the *Phoebe*, with two other families related to Martha. The Phoebe arrived in Port Adelaide on 27th March 1847. Martha and Richard's first child, the first of fourteen, was born in Kensington, now a suburb of Adelaide on 2nd September 1847. At the time of Martha's death there were fifty-two grandchildren.

Her first born, William, is my great grandpa. He named his home in Dimboola, 'Kensington' after the place where he was born.

The same obituary notice ends with: 'The esteem in which Mrs Avery was held in the Onkaparinga district was shown by the large number of friends who followed her remains to their last resting place in the Inverbrackie Churchyard. In addition to the carriages containing members of the family, forty vehicles and several horsemen joined the procession, and a large number of mourners assembled at the grave.'

Martha's dad died when she was very young. At the time of her marriage she was a domestic/house servant. Martha could read and write. She signed her marriage certificate with her name. Richard signed with a X.

If moving half-way around the world on a wooden sailing ship and farewelling family and friends she would most likely never see again was daunting, Martha was not alone. She was newly married and had family who were sharing not only the hopes of a better place but sharing the grief for those they left behind.

Martha was fortunate to be able to read and write. It meant she could write home and read the letters those at home wrote to her. It may be months and months from posting a letter until a reply is received but Martha had the capacity to maintain the connection with home.

Martha also had the support of a sister and brother. They too settled in the area of the Adelaide Hills, which Martha and Richard chose as their new home. In many ways this particular area of settlement was very like an English village. The Inverbrackie Churchyard is in the grounds of what was a Presbyterian Church. Cemeteries in Australia are rarely attached to a Church. Even today, driving through Woodside one is reminded of an English village or perhaps I should say Scottish village, for Woodside and Inverbrackie were settled by Scotsmen, hence the Presbyterian Church.

For many, coming to Australia was like coming to an alien place almost the opposite to what they called home. Families clustered together like Richard and Martha, James and his wife, Hannah and Ezra and their children. The adults, when overwhelmed with their new environment, had familiar faces to turn to, adults who understood how they felt, who could connect to the place they called home. The young children taken from the familiarity of grandparents, aunts, uncles and cousins still had some who were familiar to them and as new children were born, the new world would overtake the old.

Those who spoke the same language, shared the same accented speech, the same denominations of the Christian faith, those with similar cultural experiences or from the same land clustered or huddled together. When one is a very long way away from home, when there is nothing that reminds one of home, there is a sense of security, a sense of belonging, to huddle together with those who share a common thread. If one cannot make the new place look like the old one can name new places after the old. Woodside, Inverbrackie, Balhannah, Lobethal, Adelaide, Kensington – if the plough Richard walked behind behaved differently in Australian soil, if the Aboriginal men on the nearby hill danced in a way he didn't understand he knew at the end of the day he would go home to Martha and their children to their first child born in Kensington, the others at Woodside.

For Martha, she knew her brother and sister were in close proximity, when her labour pains began, she knew she had women she trusted to be with her during those long hours until a child was born. She knew each child would be baptised in the Inverbrackie Church where the hymns were familiar hymns, the prayers were in words she understood; as she sat and listened to Bible readings and sermons, she knew those at home would be sitting and listening in the churches of her growing up. I wonder if Martha, finding the one time she could sit still with a growing family was when she attended Church, noticed the cornerstones of the walls and keystones of the arched windows as I did as I stood amidst the ruins of the Church she once attended. Sometimes in ruins the significance of the way a structure is built is more obvious. It was in the ruins of the house Richard and Martha's first born, William, built outside Jamestown that the importance of the cornerstones when building was obvious. It was amidst the ruins of the little Church at Inverbrackie I appreciated the significance of the keystone in creating the arch of a window or door. Considering Martha's faith, she would have understood the Biblical significance of cornerstones and keystones.

As I contemplate the early settlers huddling and gathering together with like-minded early settlers, I think of those who are newly arrived in Australia today. We talk of assimilation and integration, of learning 'our' language, of 'being' Australian; becoming 'like us'. I can understand Vietnamese living in close proximity to one another, likewise Sudanese and Chinese, each culture has its own language and its own food, its own way of dressing and possibly religion. When the world around you is unfamiliar in every way there is comfort and security in huddling with those who understand what you are experiencing.

I don't like the idea of a melting pot where we all get mixed together. I've taught children of faiths other than my Christian faith, discovered our similarities and differences, I've taught children whose first language was not English, when parents struggled to understand the Australian education system, I learnt not only about the system these parents were familiar with but learnt the value of listening, of compassion and caring for those newly arrived, I also learnt the possibilities of the value of the system these people had come. The man at the Chinese Temple in Darwin broadened my mind to his faith of Tao. From the adherents of Buddhism to those of Islam, those who look beyond to Wicca; each open my eyes to something new and different.

The base language of Australia is English and an expectation of newcomers to learn English is not unreasonable, but every language has its rhythm, its patterns. The literature born of each language reflects such rhythms and patterns. I don't want us all to be mixed together for it is in our differences the fabric of our society maintains its texture and colour. Just as our landscape is rich in diversity – from deserts to tropical rain forests to the cold of Tasmania – so I appreciate the richness in the diversity of our people.

If we consider those who settled in Australia in the first fifty years of white people settlement, it may have been British rule but those who came were from many lands. The British in themselves – the Scots, the Irish, the Cornish and those within the various counties had different traditions, different accents. How easy it is to talk of the differences of those who settled in Australia yet at the same time we are pushing our indigenous people to the margins ignoring the implications of our settlement on those who have called this land home for thousands upon thousands of years.

But where does Martha fit into all this?

Mrs Avery was held in high esteem. The community of Woodside/Inverbrackie had been her home for forty-eight years. Almost double the time Martha had lived in England before migrating. To be held in high esteem Martha must have been known within the community, known as more than a wife and mother. What was she involved in? Did she belong to any groups or organisations? Perhaps in settling in a raw, just developing, area she was part of ensuring a sense of community for the women of the area.

As I've learnt more and more about each of my great, great grandmas, I've come to appreciate that many of these women were not faithful followers of their husbands but willing participants in the journey. The reality of the dream wasn't always what they expected: the heat, the flies, the loneliness, the droughts, the floods, the green never as lush as England's green, the babies lost, the children who never made it to adulthood. Martha could read and write. Did she read the letters from home for those who couldn't read? Did she write letters home for those who couldn't write? Did she welcome newcomers to their village? Was she there for women in childbirth, those who lost a baby or a growing child, perhaps a husband injured or killed?

History books tell us little about women like Martha. They are invisible between the lines on the page, even educated women like Martha. But, these women understood the need to gather together, to bond as a community, to support one another. They knew there was power in their community of women, their resilience was strengthened. As the 'nurturing' sex they were aware of community needs in a way their husbands weren't.

You won't find her name in history books but Mrs Richard Avery, my great, great grandma, was held in high esteem. She wasn't just a survivor who followed her husband across the oceans, she embraced this land and thrived. In doing so, she bonded with others walking the same path, building a community together.

History may have ignored women's work. My great, great grandma,

Mrs Richard Avery, was one of those many women. Yet, as I read her obituary I was silently shouting 'her name is Martha, her name is Martha. She was married to Richard, but her name is Martha'.

MY GREAT, GREAT, GREAT GRANDMAS

Dear Mum,

We talked about our female ancestors many times. One thing we didn't talk about though was the hidden talents of these women. Grandma (Dad's mum) wanted to study music. I believe you would have liked to have studied to be an accountant. It was money, or lack of, which meant neither of you fulfilled the career dreams you had.

Where did Grandma's love of music come from? Where did your interest in bookkeeping come from? We don't know what any of our other female forebears would have chosen as career paths had they been a young person today.

When I think of Mary, I wonder had she been at school when I was at school would she have chosen to follow a career working with children just as I wonder if Kate may have done so too. On her journey to Australia the Ship's Surgeon selected Mary to assist his wife with the children, as 'Governess', so the family story goes. Of the nearly two hundred women on the Garland Grove what qualities did sixteen-year-old Mary have making him choose her over women more experienced with young children? Mary filled this role for the complete journey. Had she not been suitable there were plenty of women who could have taken her place.

Kate, on telling her employers of her intention to get married, was asked to reconsider. They didn't want to lose her from their employ, she was so very good with the children. Kate chose to marry and have her own children. From the stories I've heard she was a very good and much-loved mum and grandma. I'm sure you agree with that Mum, having experienced her warmth and caring.

It is very easy to dismiss these two women as just doing what women do in nurturing young children. But these children were not their own and Mary was only sixteen. I'm not sure how old Kate was when she started working for the Moggs family and how long she actually worked for them. There is a vast difference between nurturing the children you have given birth to or within your immediate family circle and those you may work with beyond the home.

Is my choice to be a kindergarten teacher an inherited passion from these two women?

Is my love of writing an inherited passion from Irish Mary who entertained her family telling stories? She was illiterate so never committed her stories to paper, but her love of storytelling lives on.

We'll never know, will we Mum? Women's work was rarely recognised. All the local history books I have read say the same thing – the author cannot find any records of what women did. Women were invisible, their work unimportant so any career ambitions they may have had, if they dared consider anything beyond the bounds of the family home, were never recorded and possibly never discussed. It was more important for boys to be educated than girls.

Yet, surprises appear sometimes. Stonehenge Ann born in 1840, whose father died when she was three could read and write. Martha (Mrs Richard Avery) born 1824 could read and write. The female and male children of illiterate women who made the journey to Australia learnt to read and write.

What talents did these women have? Did they channel their talents/ skills into hobbies or community activities? The Hancock sisters were known for their music and recitation presentations at Church and community social events.

It is an area we will never know the answers to – what these women would have chosen for a career had they been born today. But it gives us something to think about, doesn't it Mum?

Love,

Judith

20
Mary Murphy (Hall)
1825 -1894

As I begin on those in my Great, Great, Great Grandmas generation who arrived in Australia, none of this generation Australian born, the gap between their life experiences and mine is vast. I often felt pity for my ancestors as their lives were tough and harsh. But the toughness and harshness needs to be viewed in the context of the time. In two hundred years how will my descendants view my lifestyle?

Time separates me from my female forebears but as I gather their stories, learn a little more of the times in which they lived, I sense the wisdom of their living connecting us. Time may separate, but a little bit of each of these women is within me. Just as I learnt much from my mum, my grandmas and Auntie through the way they lived their lives I am learning much from my female forebears in the way they lived their lives.

Looking back, I embrace the imperfections of my female forebears, admire their tenacity when they could have given up, ponder their resilience when life slops the unpalatable on their plate and open my eyes to search for the intangible creating their ability to bungy jump through life. I doubt these women want my pity, rather for me to see their lives were worthwhile even when the journey was a little rough.

Mary was probably born in Ireland. Her convict record states she was 'brought up in Bristol' implying she was not born in Bristol.

In the later part of 1841 Mary was caught, along with her friend, Mary Ball, attempting to steal material. They were charged with theft. My Mary was found guilty, her friend Mary Ball was found not guilty. My Mary was sentenced to four months hard labour in Bristol prison. She served her time over the Christmas period in the depths of an English winter. I initially felt dismay at the fear Mary must have experienced during the trial in October 1841. But Mary chose to attempt to represent herself. An illiterate kitchen maid would have few skills to bring to the court room and little knowledge or experience of court room procedure. But attempt to represent herself she did. A short article in the Bristol Times and Mirror of 30 October 1841 titled 'The Bag. Bristol Quarter Sessions' states:

'Mary Ball and Mary Murphy was indicted for stealing a quantity of cotton goods from the shop of Richard Warr. The prisoners were without the assistance of counsel, and their appearance exciting considerable interest around the Bar table, Mr Stone, as the senior barrister present was requested by his learned juniors to undertake the defence gratuitously. He was so kind as to comply with their wish, and we need not say that he afforded another instance of his exquisite legal subtlety, and again displayed his dazzling eloquence. He succeeded in obtaining a verdict of acquittal in favour of prisoner Ball, but the case of Murphy was hopeless, as she was detected in the very act of taking.' The remainder of the short article relates to the story of the bag. I suspect the legal fraternity may have had quite a laugh at the Marys expense, but I wish, I really wish, there was greater detail about 'their appearance exciting considerable interest around the bar table'. What was it that excited considerable interest? Their clothing, their manner? I can only imagine how Mary felt on being found guilty but somehow, through the words of an old newspaper article I've developed quite an admiration for the illiterate kitchen maid.

About three months after her release from Bristol prison my Mary was again caught, along with her friend Mary Ball, attempting to steal material. They were again charged with theft. My Mary was found guilty again. A second conviction was generally a transportation sentence. Mary received seven years. Her friend, Mary Ball was found not guilty again. Mary's occupation on her convict records on her first offence was 'kitchen maid'. On her second offence, 'on the town'. I wondered why my Mary was not charged with prostitution. Apparently, if a woman has a place to live and works as a prostitute she may be charged with prostitution. Mary however was homeless, living on a public street she was basically public property. However we may judge people like Mary she was sixteen years old, had a prison record, with no home and no job, the only commodity she had to sell to earn money to live was to sell her own body.

On October 2nd, 1842 the convict ship Garland Grove left Woolwich with Mary on board. In the first few days she was treated for gonorrhoea. The story woven in Mary's fabric within our family story is that she was the governess to the children of the ship's surgeon. I think governess is rather an embellished word for an illiterate sixteen-year-old. Obviously, the surgeon knew Mary's background but there must have been something about her making him select her to assist his wife in caring for their children on the voyage. It is in his final remarks about Mary at the end of the voyage I know I have discovered gold, 'a giddy girl but has a remarkable good memory and with care may turn out well'. After all that has happened to Mary, she is still 'a giddy girl' and perhaps 'giddy girls' don't always think of the consequences of their actions and that is what led to her stealing. It makes me a little sad when reading this for I know what happens to Mary in the next fifty years before her death. There was much yet to come that will test her 'giddy nature' but then again, I only see the recorded entries in official records, I'm not able to be part of the everyday when the 'giddy girl' may have had much to celebrate.

After her arrival in Van Diemen's land on January 20, 1843 little is recorded about Mary, obviously she curbed her 'giddiness' enough to keep out of trouble. In 1844 she applied for permission to marry, which was granted. In October of that year she married James Hall, a free man in Launceston. In 1845 she received her Ticket of Leave and was granted her freedom in 1849. We know Mary and James had at least two children in Tasmania; only one can be found in the records. The next time we find them is at Cavendish, near Hamilton in western Victoria. Quite possibly they caught a local coastal ship to Geelong or

Portland and made their way to Cavendish. On his death certificate James is listed as a timber sawyer. Cavendish was known as red gum country; an ideal place for a timber sawyer to stay awhile.

James and Mary were not particularly conscientious about reporting the births of their children, or maybe, it was just too far to go to wherever they needed to go, or maybe we just haven't found the records yet. Two births have been recorded. Phoebe, born in 1853, is in the South Australian records. For some years that invisible line separating Victoria and South Australia moved from time to time due to political bickering. Phoebe's birth is part of the history of that moving line. George, born in 1855, is in Victorian records. The informant was a Police Sergeant from Hamilton. I am assuming the Police Sergeant made a trip to Cavendish recording the births of children whose parents did not or could not make the journey to Hamilton to do it themselves. Sadly, James and Mary had also lost children. These are not recorded either. Perhaps there were local records which never made it to official places. The deaths of small babies and children must have been a sadness that tested the 'giddy girl'.

In 1856 James' name appears on a large advertisement in a local paper as having applied to vote in Victorian Legislative Council elections. To be eligible to vote the voter had to own land. James may have owned only a very small portion of land but possibly it was land with a dwelling for his growing family.

The family moved to Ararat towards the end of the 1850s. Once again children's births and deaths have not been recorded or the records not found. In November 1860 James died, of an 'abscess of the hand', according to his death certificate. When I first discovered this, it seemed a reasonable occurrence. A timber sawyer would often experience cuts and scratches and it would be easy for these to get infected. Infections can lead to more serious infections which can lead to death. James was thirty-eight years old. There are eight children listed on his death certificate. The eldest fifteen. The youngest one.

For a couple of weeks after James' death the local Ararat paper carried large articles about accusations against the local hospital and a lack of care in relation to James. To be admitted to hospital, in the era of James' death, one had to be a subscriber, which James wasn't. However, a subscriber or doctor could authorise admittance. This was done. James attended as requested but admittance was only on certain days of the week. James didn't attend on the correct day. At the public enquiry the hospital administrators claimed no one was ever turned away even if they turned up for admittance on the wrong day. There was much he said, they said, James said and so forth as there is in such enquiries. James was 'painted' in colours that did him no benefit. He was a sly grog shop owner, which no one denied. It was claimed he didn't want to be admitted because it was the end of the shearing season and he wanted to be home 'because the old woman didn't know what to do'.

Sly grog shops are not exactly elite establishments. Thirsty shearers at the end of the shearing season are not always polite customers. Mary, present at the inquiry, had a 'babe in arms'. At James death she was either heavily pregnant or had a very young baby. James talk may have been rough talk but at the same time Mary was possibly not in the best position to deal with impolite customers.

Mary was called as a witness as was their thirteen-year-old son John. When a doctor repeated what he claimed Mary had said to him about how much James drank, the implication was James was an alcoholic, Mary denied ever saying that. Her denial carried little weight. As I read the article I was internally shouting across the years, 'she had a remarkable good memory'. But there was no one to listen to me as there was no one to listen to Mary. The inquiry concluded the hospital was not to blame. James had died the day after being 'refused' admittance. The eight mile walk home may have sped up his death but his death from consumption was imminent as the doctor and Mary already knew. I suspect there was a degree of negligence on the hospital's part. As a timber sawyer and maybe as part of his personality he was rough and abrupt. He was also an extremely sick man and had been for some months. He could no longer earn a living as a timber sawyer, but he could as a sly grog shop owner. The doctor who denied any wrongdoing on the part of the hospital in relation to James' care was the same doctor who treated James over the months and certified James died of an 'abscess on the hand' when he in fact had died of consumption.

Mary now had eight children to not only care for but feed. I think the eldest, at fifteen, was working but probably not earning enough to keep a family. In the March after James died Mary was charged with shoplifting, along with two men. The two men pleaded guilty and were sentenced to prison terms. Mary pleaded not guilty and went to trial. She was found guilty and sentenced to twelve months in a Melbourne gaol. While she was in custody her children were left with no one to care for them. They were charged with vagrancy. The judge said he didn't think he could charge such young children with vagrancy, but he did. The children were held in custody with Mary. It was a wise judge who made such decision. The children went with Mary to the Melbourne gaol. On their release they returned to Ararat to Mary's eldest. The family reunited again. Mary had two more children on her return. Their births are not recorded but on their death certificates James is listed as their father on at least one of the certificates! Did Mary have a new partner, or did she return to that oldest profession as the only way she could to support her family?

While Mary was in the Melbourne gaol her term was extended for a few days for the use of 'improper language'. The language she used is not noted but I gather it was more appropriate around a sly grog shop than in the local library.

When Mary's daughter Phoebe was married Mary signed the marriage certificate giving permission for her seventeen-year-old daughter to marry. Normally a father would have done this, but James had already died. In many circumstances an adult brother would have done this. Phoebe had adult brothers, but it was her mother Mary who signed with a X. The 'giddy' girl displaying feminist tendencies before the word had been invented.

From my calculations Mary gave birth to at least thirteen children, perhaps more. At the time of her death at the age of sixty-nine only five were still living. Mary cared for most of these who died at home. None of the children of Mary and James chose lifestyles outside the law. They were respected in their local community. Some had obituaries in the local paper acknowledging the jobs they had held. They were spoken of as hardworking, decent people.

Mary is buried in the Ararat cemetery with three of her sons and a grandchild. In the plot beside hers another two sons are buried as well as two grandchildren. The railing around Mary's grave is rusted and on a lean. The once splendid gravestone is in need of repair. Her name is still clear for passersby to read as are those of her sons. James, her husband, was buried in the old Ararat cemetery. A factory was built over the old cemetery, which burnt down. It is now an unkempt vacant block bounded on three sides with pines.

When I first started planning 'Inherited Touch' I intended to call it 'A Cup of Tea with Grandma' working the stories of the women around an imagined afternoon tea with all my female forebears invited. As I contemplated the logistics, I realised it was beyond this writer's capabilities. I also became well aware of the number of quite strong-willed women who lived before me. An afternoon tea of guests with the potential of personality clashes was one I wasn't sure I was capable of controlling. From staunch Methodist Great Grandma Charlotte with her white-gloved guests to Catholic Gr. Gr. Gr. Grandma Mary with a prison record and the widow of a sly grog seller I took cover, giving each of my female forebears her own chapter in the book. Yet, part of me would like to be witness to the meeting of Charlotte and Mary. Two formidable women appearing to have little in common, yet both devoted to family, remembered for their devotion. If I scrape away the veneer society has coated each with, dust off the box society has placed each one in, I may well discover two women with much in common. I may well discover two women sharing stories of their children, their grandchildren, and the small towns they came to call home. I was brought up within the Methodist tradition as Great Grandma Charlotte was, yet, my mum (who is the thread connecting me to Mary), although a strong Methodist, had no qualms about being a neighbour to staunch Catholics.

I am descended from a number of people buried in Ararat cemetery and visit from time to time to research. Each time I stand in front of Mary's grave with its splendid memorial erected by her children I ponder the journey of an illiterate kitchen maid to the gold mining town of Ararat.

The Ship's Surgeon on the convict ship the *Garland Grove* wrote, 'with care could turn out well'. I think Mary did more of the caring than being cared for but thinking about the fine, decent children Mary never once deserted, whatever life dealt her I'd think the Ship's Surgeon would agree, Mary did indeed turn out well.

21
Sarah Bowtell (Clark)
1818 - 1895

Sarah was counting the hours until the ship docked in Geelong. *Not long until we walk on firm land again*, she thought, as the soon-to-be-born child she was carrying fought the confines of her womb. *Is that a hand or a foot?* she wondered, her own hand resting on the moving infant within. She gave a silent prayer of thanks for a healthy pregnancy, for the seven healthy children accompanying her and Leonard on this journey. 'Please God', the prayer continued, 'let this baby be born healthy and may it thrive in this new land'. Before Amen could conclude her prayer the ship lurched and rocked ... Sarah cradling her swollen belly reached for Eli, the youngest of their seven.

About the 2nd/3rd May 1854 the ship *America* ran aground as it approached Geelong. The ship remained upright but was firmly entrenched in the earth beneath the ocean. Children and women were taken from the ship and transported to emergency accommodation in Geelong. The America was eventually freed arriving in Geelong on 4th May. It is an interesting anecdote to include in Sarah's story. But I can only imagine Sarah's fear at being taken from the ship with her children, leaving Leonard on board. There was no gangplank to walk down. I assume those being evacuated were lowered over the side of the ship to waiting vessels below, hardly an easy task for an over eight-month-pregnant woman. Sarah also had little children to take care for. She gave birth to their eighth child on 20th May in Geelong. I know very little about Sarah's personality, but I have to admire her tenacity and strength in what would have been overwhelming circumstances.

Gr. Gr. Gr. Grandma Sarah was born in 1818 in Barley in the county of Hertfordshire in England. She married Leonard when she was seventeen. Was mother to seven children when they migrated to Australia in 1854. A mother to another four children by the time she died in 1895 at Cathcart outside Ararat. Sarah was eighteen when she gave birth to her first child, forty-five years of age when she gave birth to her last. At the time of her death Sarah had been a widow for eighteen years.

It is difficult today to imagine having children over such a large number of years. As Sarah was giving birth to her last child, her older children were married and giving birth to their own children. The generations overlapped, interconnected and family history researchers often have difficulty sorting out which generation is which particularly when families recycled names through the generations. There was a security, a safety-net in large families. Older siblings helped care for younger siblings, women learnt about childbirth and raising children, not from ante-natal classes common today, but from practical experience in helping their own mothers or aunts or big sisters if they were the little sisters. They were also supported in their pregnancies, childbirth and child rearing. Supported too in the death of a child as this was sadly a commonplace event. If a mother or father died with a young family, there were other family members who could step in to help. Cousins grew up together, the extended family a community in itself. When parents became older there was always family who would take them in and care for them in their later years. It wasn't uncommon for three generations to be sharing a home. Young children learnt to appreciate and respect the older generation. This may well be the 'ideal' which obviously, knowing the varying natures of human beings, may be far from the truth. But, nevertheless, although a generalisation it was what many families attempted to fulfil.

I may look back with dismay on the role women were confined to in the era when Sarah was a young woman. But that sense of community, that sense of belonging, that sense of security within the extended family has its advantages. Women may have lacked freedom to enter the workforce or follow a career path when families were large, but they didn't lack opportunity to be part of a female community.

When families, such as Sarah and Leonard chose to migrate, Sarah left behind her female community, her support base, her security-net. It also meant she left behind her parents and siblings. In their later years she would not be available to support her parents. This disconnection by choice created new needs in the non-indigenous communities in Australia.

Sarah and Leonard were employed in advance of their arrival in Australia to a property in East Geelong for three months and the four older girls in positions close by. It was a security-net knowing they had work and a home on arrival. They moved from Geelong after about six months to Ararat to Burrumbeep Station. Gold had been discovered at Burrumbeep in 1854. Leonard was a miner originally but became the 'first gardener' on the Station at a later stage. Over the years he is noted as a miner, gardener, labourer and farmer. Ten of Sarah and Leonard's children married and had families of their own.

In 1907, there were jubilee celebrations in Ararat recognising the fiftieth anniversary of the opening of Canton Lead.

In 1857 Chinese miners journeying to the Clunes gold fields stopped at a spring to replenish their water supplies unexpectedly discovering Canton Lead, what would become the world's richest shallow alluvial goldfield. Originally called Canton Lead it became Mount Ararat then simply Ararat. It is the only city in Australia to be founded by Chinese immigrants. In recent years, a section of the Ararat cemetery where many Chinese are buried has been renovated acknowledging the contribution the Chinese have made to Ararat.

In 1907, the men who were pioneers in 1857 or their sons, were planning a celebration of the opening of Canton Lead. A civic leader James Tuson felt all the women who had been 'pioneers' should be included. This apparently didn't happen, but Mr Tuson organised an afternoon tea for the pioneer ladies. Five of Sarah and Leonard's daughters were invited. Two of the daughters who attended, Sarah and Mary, spoke at the gathering. At the time Mr Tuson said these two sisters represented a family of 220. Mary talked of the *America* running aground and being taken off the boat in the middle of the night. Sarah remembered the eleven-day trip by bullock dray from Geelong to Ararat. The drays were strong but not known for comfort. They were pulled by ten or twelve bullocks.

It is interesting to note men were considered pioneers, but the women were not. A 'thumbs ups' would have to go to Mr Tuson for acknowledging the women. It is also interesting to note the Chinese do not appear to have been represented. The very people who discovered the gold, birthing what is now known as Ararat, were not considered pioneers either.

I feel a sense of inadequacy in knowing so little of Sarah, of the type of person she was, the type of mother, her community involvement. Women's stories are generally silent stories, told amongst women they stay amongst the women who shared them, rarely recorded. Women's work of little significance yet it is women in bringing up the children (for bringing up children was woman's work) who would have instilled in the children life values and ethics, who would have instilled in boys a respect for women and commitment to work, who would have instilled in girls a sense of female connectedness and community. It was women who supported their husbands to enable them to do the work they did. I'm not sure Sarah thought of all this. I'm not sure Sarah tugged at the confinement women experienced in her era. Perhaps she accepted the role of women and was happy with it. Maybe she was too busy to think beyond where she was at. But somehow, I'm sure Sarah, who sailed half-way around the world was not a meek woman following her husband's commands. Nearly full-term pregnant Sarah aground on the sand on the *America*, being taken from the *America* to a safe place until the ship refloats and docks in Geelong waiting for her husband to reach land is not a weak woman. She may have been very afraid in the circumstances, but fear is not a weakness. I'm not sure what Sarah thought, only Sarah knows that. I may know little about Sarah but Sarah and Leonard's children thrived in this land of their parents choosing. Resilience cannot be taught or learnt, it is experienced in negotiating life's smooth surfaces and bumpy roads. Sarah, as a mother, must have hugged her children close enough for them to feel safe, yet gave them enough space to experience the rockiness, to develop the resilience to not only survive but thrive as Sarah had done in migrating to Australia.

Sarah died on July 29, 1895. Her death notice reads 'Passed away quietly at her late residence ...' Sarah died at home and perhaps the wording 'passed away quietly' reflects her personality. She may have been a woman who did not seek the limelight. Twelve months later her family insert another notice, 'In loving remembrance of our dear mother, Sarah Clark, who fell asleep 29 July 1895. Inserted by her children.'

22
Mary Ann Kay (Kain)
1823 – 1870

In its early days Coober Pedy was known as the town to go to if you wanted to disappear. Well over 45 nationalities populated the area at one stage. Countless mine shafts may hide those 'assisted' in disappearing. At census time many residents simply didn't fill in the forms or if they did no one really knew if the information was fact or fiction, so population statistics were never accurate.

However, it is possible to disappear, or at least be invisible, amidst more populated areas. Mary Ann is one who by choice or simply by living on the edge of society has become invisible. My knowledge of Gr. Gr. Gr. Grandma Mary Ann is almost a dot-point single page document.

- Mary Ann was 27 when she married in Adelaide in 1848 to a John Woodall. Her maiden name on the marriage certificate was Kain.

- Obviously Mary Ann and John came from somewhere but somewhere is rather a large place containing many locations and very few maps to guide the journey.

Inherited Touch

- Mary Ann and John left few footprints other than the birth/baptism details of their ten children. Their first child born in Adelaide another at Pine Hills (a property near Harrow) three children baptised at Lake Wallace where John was a shepherd, their journey ending outside Ararat in a gold mining area where the last of the children were born. Mary Ann's maiden name where shown on their children's birth records varies – Kame, Kann, Kain, Kane.

- When their daughter Jane (my Gr. Gr. Grandma) married in 1867 Mary Ann's maiden name is written as Kay.

- One of Mary Ann's daughters drowns in a dam on their property. There is an inquest into the cause of her death written up in the local paper.

- John's name appears in the local paper on a few occasions usually regarding altercations with members of the Chinese community.

- Mary Ann dies in 1870 in the Ararat hospital. She had an 'abscess in brain' and had been ill for four months. Her death certificate states her parents were 'unknown', but she came from Cornwall. John was the informant, but no children are listed, although '10 children' was added later. It states Mary Ann arrived in Australia about 1846-47 and had been in Victoria 23 years. The local paper at that time listed all those who had died in the Ararat Hospital that week. Mary Ann Woodall came from St Anstle in Cornwall, according to the paper. I'm assuming St Anstle could be St Austell. Mary Ann is buried in an unmarked grave in the Ararat cemetery.

- Was Mary Ann a survivor or did she thrive in what I perceive to be a tough and inhospitable environment?

- Mary Ann and John would have travelled from Adelaide to Pine Hills to Lake Wallace when the land was in many ways a virgin land, with only minor impressions of white people's imprint. Neither of them was Australian born. The landscapes of their birth in vast contrast to those they now walked upon. I suspect Mary Ann may have been illiterate, but John signed his name as informant on Mary Ann's death certificate. Part of me would have loved walking with them to view the land before it became farmland, to have met or seen the indigenous people before they were forced to the margins of Australian history.

- If Mary Ann arrived about 1846-47 as was calculated on her death certificate when she would have been in her early twenties she possibly arrived alone, a young woman with a dream, with hopes. What did she leave behind? Who did she leave behind? However tough it may have been economically it is still home and leaving it would have been difficult, just as the journey would have been filled with anticipation of something better and fear of the unknown. What did Mary Ann do once she arrived here? How did John and Mary Ann travel across unfamiliar and almost unmarked land with a young family? So many sentences ending in a question mark? So many empty lines stalking the question marks with more questions?

I struggle to find a sense of Mary Ann. When her fourteen-month old daughter is drowned in the dam the clinical nature in the reporting of the inquest pushes any emotion aside. It is almost as cold as the poor dead child. It is only when I let myself hear the fearful cries of one sister calling the older sister, 'Jane, Jane' after pulling the drowned child from the dam I sense the trauma of the event. I hear sticks crack as Jane runs across the ground gathering up the lifeless body in her arms running to her brother at the other end of the dam her shoes and feet attempting to maintain her balance along the roughened edges of the dam. Jane leaving the lifeless, dripping body in her brother's arms as she gains speed along a rough bush track, lungs heaving and heart pounding to arrive at Mrs McKay's where her mother was, breathless words breaking the news. Mary Ann running, running, running back along the track, breathless Jane attempting to keep up, Mrs Mckay running with them, until Mary Ann takes her daughter's body from her son crumpling to sit on the crusted dam edge clutching the small limp body of her daughter Amelia to her. Amidst this sad scenario I find an essence of Mary Ann.

Her friend, Mrs Mckay is with her. No one could take away Mary Ann's pain and sorrow, but another woman can empathise, can sit with her as she cries, can tell the other children what to do next, comfort the other children when Mary Ann is too distraught to do so. Jane, at fourteen years of age, is not a little girl. As they gather around their mother, she becomes a mothering figure. 'We live in the shelter of one another.' The news would have spread amongst the mining settlement. Others would have lost children in varying circumstances. In the rough, often uncouth environment of a mining settlement there were others who understood the sorrow. Where was John in all this? I don't know. Sometimes the death of a child is woman's work, woman's sorrow. This is not to say men did not grieve but women, at least in death, had a freedom to grieve more openly than men did. Mary Ann and John's children had manners. Jane referred to their neighbour as Mrs McKay. Her manners may not have been of the standard for ladies afternoon tea parties but she had been taught the basics. She referred to her elder as Mrs Mckay.

When I think of Mary Ann, I recall my health hiccup with breast cancer. I call it a hiccup now; at the time it was a little scary. I'm not sure why I recall it with Mary Ann as her life and mine were very different. However, in the sad event of the drowning of her daughter Amelia, Mary Ann had her friend Mrs McKay. Had she suffered the loss of a child? The gold fields and the times were not kind to parents with young children. I don't know the statistics, but possibly more women had experienced the death of a child than those who had not. Mary Ann would grieve but she would not have grieved alone. When I had breast cancer, I joined a Support Group, the Luminaries. There was great comfort in being with a group of women who were walking the same path as I was, who understood how I felt. Being part of such a group we knew some would have fewer years than others but none of us walked the path alone. We 'lived in the shelter of one another' as Mary Ann 'lived in the shelter of others'.

Six years later Mary Ann is dead, the youngest of the ten children still not old enough to care for themselves. Who cared for them following Mary Ann's death?

Eight years after Mary Ann died, John died of cancer of the stomach. He remarried after Mary Ann's death and had three more children with his second wife. His daughter Maud, from his first marriage was the informant on his death. He died in Horsham. Did the youngest children go with him in the move to Horsham? Was Maud living with him and his second wife helping with the young children? 'We live in the shelter of one another.'

Gr. Gr. Gr. Grandma Mary Ann may be invisible in the pages of history books. Her journey lost in the layers of dust as she journeyed across the plains of Western Victoria, muted in the depths of the gold field mine shafts. Her journey across the oceans has been washed from the maps. But journey she did. Survive she did. But did she thrive? I'd like to think she felt she'd thrived, or perhaps that isn't the way she thought of life. She chose to journey searching for something better.

Looking backwards as I am, I may wonder if the journey was worth it, but despite the roughness and toughness it may well be Mary Ann was pleased with her decision. As I feel the strength of her thread in the family cloth, I sense the essence of her presence, a yearning to continue the search adding substance to her story. Gr. Gr. Gr. Grandma Mary Ann is worthy of the effort.

23
Charlotte Foote (Smart)
1820 -1889

It was the end of a long but happy day exploring parts of Cornwall before venturing into Somerset, but we couldn't find the Church in Compton Pauncefoot where Charlotte and her husband Richard were baptised and married. The narrow streets and roads along with the unfamiliar territory of an overseas holiday exacerbated our tiredness. 'I've seen the village,' I said, 'I'm satisfied with that, we won't waste any more time looking. It's time to drive to the next town where we will stay the night.' As Michael backed around, the street too narrow for a U-turn, he saw in the rear-view mirror a spire stretching above the trees. We'd found the Church. More exciting was to walk in the door and find a small history book written in recent years detailing information about Charlotte and Richard and Richard's brother and his wife who came out to Australia on the same ship, the *Lalla Rookh*, in 1840. Further delight to discover information, in the same little book of other family members who had worshipped in the little church.

A church building is only a building, it is the people, the worshipping community who create a church. Yet, there is a presence in an empty church one doesn't necessarily feel elsewhere. God is not confined to a building, God is present on the dirtiest street corner, the roughest pub, the remotest corner of the Kimberleys as much as he is in a consecrated church building. But the symbols, the specific furniture of pulpit, baptismal font and communion areas create an atmosphere of worship. We'd visited many village churches on our holiday as I explored the little places some of my ancestors had come from, each of them rich with centuries of worshipping communities. As I thought of the church we attended, the people we sat with each week I could feel a connection of faith through the generations. A connection of faith as I connected with Roman Catholics, Anglicans, Methodists, Presbyterians, within my family history, perhaps there are others I have yet to discover. That morning we had been to the Witchcraft Museum at Boscastle. There too I had discovered the weaving of Christianity, Witchcraft, Wicca through the broader interpretation of religion over the centuries. The natural world with all its complexities and wonder to the wise women of the villages who understood the healing power of herbs and natural elements, the many definitions of God were curling around one another. We each follow a different path but there's a wonderful sense of belonging when the paths criss-cross from time to time, the smell of herbs or the dazzling of Artemis' robes, the meaning of stones in an ancient place to the church building I sat in as Gr. Gr. Gr. Grandma had sat in so long ago, from a new born as her parents presented her for baptism to the day she made vows to 'love, honour and cherish'. The day had been long, I was tired, but in the confines of that church with all I had seen and experienced in that day whirling around in my mind I felt a sense of peace. I felt a connection not only with Charlotte who made the choice to trust beyond the familiar but to those who came before her who had called Compton Pauncefoot their home.

I marvel at these women who sailed the oceans for many, many weeks in wooden sailing vessels. They farewelled family and friends, the community and landscapes that were home for an unknown, but hopefully, better future in another land. It appears Richard and Charlotte landed first in Adelaide then to Tasmania where their first two children were born before returning to Adelaide and Hindmarsh (now an inner suburb of Adelaide) to the goldfields in the Adelaide hills where more children were born but sadly not all survived to travel with the family from the Adelaide hills to the goldfields of

Ararat where the last of their children were born.

Charlotte was born in 1820. She married Richard on 5th April 1840. Richard signed his name on the marriage certificate, Charlotte signed with a X. On 26th April 1840 they set sail on the *Lalla Rookh* arriving in Adelaide on 11th August of the same year. On his marriage certificate Richard is listed as a tiler and on death certificate as a plasterer. In between his marriage and death, he was more often listed as a miner.

I wonder what happened between Charlotte, Richard and their children towards the end of Richard and Charlotte's lives.

Charlotte died on 11th January 1889 of Phthisis having been ill for one year. Richard is the informant on her death certificate. Of the at least eleven children he and Charlotte had only four sons are listed on her death certificate.

Richard died on 25th November 1895 of chronic pneumonia accelerated by injuries received. A magisterial inquiry was held. The informant on Richard's death certificate was John Thompson/ Constable of Police/ Ararat/ Present at Inquiry. In the column where the names and ages of children are listed are the words – 'Ten sons living'/ 'Names & ages Not Known'.

As the hope of tomorrow shines through from my visit to the little church at Compton Pauncefoot and the sadness not necessarily of Charlotte and Richard's death, but the apparent disintegration of the family unit with so little information available for the death certificates, I wonder about all the years in between. I sense a shifting in my perceptions of telling the stories of my female forebears. If their world had gone 'belly-up' for whatever reasons in those later years does that diminish their lives in all the years before that? Does it mean Charlotte was not resilient? I think of my mum and dad. How our family unit was shredded because one member wanted control. Does that mean my mum was not resilient for all the many years before that? Does that mean my decent, honest Dad wasn't such a decent, honest person? I ponder the vulnerability of old age, the complexity of family relationships – being born, the vulnerability of childhood, growing up, the career paths we follow, the life partner/s we choose, the decisions we make, those we trust and those we love, the children we have, the unexpected highs and lows, children leaving home, getting older, the vulnerability of old age.

Is our resilience consistent through the varying ages of our living?

Can we lose, yet retrieve it? Does it come in varying shades and tastes? Is our resilience what others perceive of us or what we perceive of ourselves? Can we judge if another is/is not resilient? Can we be honest enough to judge our own resilience?

As I tell the stories of these women, my gr. gr. gr. grandmas, there is much I assume. Time has eliminated many of their stories, they risk becoming names and dates, places and connections without the pulse that keeps connections breathing. Yet, in the stories becoming lost it opens up spaces for possibility as I ponder on the greater picture of who they were and the world around them they lived in at the time.

Gr.Gr.Gr. Grandma Charlotte was a resilient woman who sailed a very long way to fulfil a dream. I'm sure there were nightmares along the way, the deaths of children, life in tents on goldfields, times when gold was scarce, but still she believed the journey was worth it. How do I know that? She got up every morning and cared for her family. Resilience isn't achieving miraculous wonders every day, sometimes it is simply finding the smallest scrap of strength to get up and face another day; believing the day, the people one will meet that day or even just believing I am worth the effort to get up and face that day. Sometimes resilience is dealing with one day at a time. If choices others made in the final years highlighted Charlotte's vulnerability in old age perhaps it also highlights the lesson of the power each of us have to nurture or to destroy the resilience of another. The power each of us has to carry some of the vulnerability thus enriching the lives of the vulnerable.

In telling Charlotte's story I cannot change her story but the strength of her thread within the family cloth weaves through the generations.

24
Eliza/Elizabeth Bickford (Boon)
1811 - 1857

When I first became the collector of stories of my female forebears, I decided to trace each line back to the woman who first arrived in Australia. While my process worked quite clearly for every line the pattern broke with Eliza or Elizabeth as she is called in some records. Gr. Gr. Gr. Grandma Eliza never came to Australia, but her parents did. I'm not sure of the exact year Eliza's parents migrated but it was well after Eliza had married her husband John. Eliza's parents left their nine living children in England and sailed to South Australia. In the years to follow many of their children made the same journey.

It takes much resilience, courage, or what is often termed intestinal fortitude, to make the decision to migrate to another land. It is usually children who make such decisions, keen to fly the nest, see new places or make their own way in the world. I wonder how Eliza and her siblings felt when their parents first told them of their plans. Some obviously were inspired by the idea and followed in their parents' footsteps, perhaps that was the intent.

Eliza and John had a young family with still more to come in the years after Eliza's parents migrated. One of their sons, my gr. gr. grandpa became a ship's carpenter and eventually migrated to Australia. By the time he migrated Eliza and John had both died.

I'm not sure if Eliza and John ever contemplated the journey to Australia. With Eliza's siblings making such a move it must have been something they at least discussed perhaps deciding it wasn't the right choice for them.

While it may take resilience, courage or intestinal fortitude in making the decision to migrate it takes the same to stay. When the family unit so many rely upon is changing it must have created an uncertainty, a questioning, amongst those choosing to stay. If there is a safety-net, a security in numbers, when those numbers decrease because some are searching further afield, when they may never be seen again, I wonder how Eliza felt.

Eliza and John's last child was born in 1850. Eliza's dad died in 1851 in South Australia, a few years after migrating with his wife, Ann. In 1854 Eliza and John's last born child died. A few weeks later John committed suicide. In 1857 Eliza died. Eliza's mum did not die until 1876.

There's a different pattern, a different texture in the family cloth, the thread I would have expected to link the last woman (Eliza's mum) in that line coming to Australia is still connected through Eliza but the thread follows a different path, a different weave. Stories cannot be confined or made to conform to a set pattern. Yet, the very changing of an expected pattern creates an uncertainty, a questioning beyond the generation in which it occurred. As the collector of the stories I accepted the decisions children made to adventure to another place, but I queried how parents could leave their children. Yet, as my husband and I have one foot in the retirement years I embrace the opportunities we have to follow other paths. I object to being labelled, being expected to conform to certain expectations because of my age or the greying of my hair.

Gr. Gr. Gr. Grandma Eliza didn't come to Australia yet her thread in the family cloth is just as strong, perhaps a little stronger when the pattern dares to be different.

25
Tamson/Thomazine/Thomasina Bray (Bishop/Boundy)
1802 - 1898

A chill wind brushes across the headstones scattered throughout the grounds of the Gwennap Church in Cornwall. William holds the door of the stone building open as Sarah steps into the familiar place of worship. As they take their seats she removes the outer shawl from the babe resting in her arms, giving a silent prayer of thanks for the healthy child, Thomasina, they are presenting for baptism today – Christmas Day 1802.

Thomasina was the fourth of six children born to William and Sarah Bray. The sixth child, named William, was born on 15th July 1807. William, the husband of Sarah and father to six children died on 16th July 1807. Sarah died in 1851. She never remarried.

I can only assume it was an extremely difficult time for Sarah raising her children without her husband to support them. It was also a difficult time for the population of Cornwall as the structures supporting the economy trembled. The once wealthy felt the trembling and the waves of financial insecurity and deprivation swept through all levels of society. Quite possibly Sarah's children joined the many other children earning a meagre income underground in the copper and tin mines of Cornwall. It is beyond my comprehension to consider these young children, the age of our children today just entering secondary school, were working six long days a week, hardly ever seeing daylight hours.

Thomasina married James Bishop on 5th August 1826. They had nine children together. Not all lived to adulthood. On the 1851 Census records James is listed as 'work in copper mine' as are his son William and daughter Lavinia. His youngest child, Joseph is a 'scholar'.

In July 1855 Thomasina received the dreaded news every wife of a copper miner knew was possible. There'd been an accident at the mine. She was now a widow. Just over twelve months later Thomasina married Thomas Boundy. Thomas' wife had died about eighteen months before. On 6th May 1857 with Thomasina's son, Joseph and Thomas's son, Thomas they set sail for Australia on the *Sumner*.

The waves of financial insecurity and deprivation had set in motion waves of emigration from Cornwall to Australia and America. Despite both being forty-seven years of age, Thomasina and Thomas chose to ride the waves. In the 1850s and 1860s siblings of Thomasina and Thomas and of their spouses buried in Cornish soil, sailed on the many ships departing England. Their adult children too were making these choices, saving as quickly as they could and booking passages on the next available ships. Thomasina was keen to see her daughter Lavinia who was now on the goldfields of Victoria with her husband and young children. The three-and-a-half-month voyage was daunting but they were not alone for they knew many who had already made the voyage and would soon be joined by those planning their own journey to Australia.

Thomasina stood at the railings beside her husband Thomas. As the land faded into the horizon Thomasine turned to Thomas and the two children standing beside them. The four of them, still unsteady on their feet in the first hours of a ship riding the swell, leant close to one another as they made their way below. On the 21st August 1857 they had to once again find their land legs as they stepped ashore in Adelaide.

The Bray, Bishop, Boundy and Hancock names, for those are the family names of my Cornish ancestors who journeyed to Australia, are amongst the many who worked the copper mines at Burra. These are part of the extended family for each chose varying paths in their new land. My direct ancestors, many of whom stepped ashore in Adelaide, followed the rapidly well-worn road to the goldfields of Victoria.

After the five to six-week journey from Adelaide to Campbell's Creek (part of the Castlemaine-Mt Alexander gold field) Thomasina and Thomas were reunited with Lavinia and Richard and their four little children. How excited the adults must have been to be together again. One can only imagine the joy and happiness. Excitement tinged with sadness as Lavinia remembered her dad killed in mines. The four little children may have been a little wary of these new adults or perhaps they too were caught up in the excitement of having grandparents in their lives. I'm sure Lavinia welcomed the help Thomasina would be so very pleased to offer her daughter and the fun she could share with her grandchildren.

Within a little over two years Lavinia and Richard had moved to Clunes where they added another eight children to their family. Thomasina and Thomas made Campbell's Creek their home. Thomas started out as a miner and appears to have been reasonably successful and active within the community. He owned a house and won prizes for his grapes at an agricultural show. He was a shareholder in a goldmine which his brother-in-law, Henry Bishop, established. Henry's wife was Thomas' sister Martha. Henry and Martha had migrated with their children. They were a long way from Cornwall but family were gathering together beyond the Cornish coast.

It is interesting to note the strong affiliation these families had with the Church of England in Cornwall but once in Australia they became staunch Methodists. The vibrant, dynamic sermons of John Wesley in the Gwennap Pit and other places of Cornwall, his message for the ordinary people and the struggles they were enduring, had settled deep within their spiritual being. They worshipped in the Methodist Church with some of the men becoming local preachers.

Churches were central to communities on the goldfields and perhaps with so many having migrated they were in many respects the family they'd left behind. When miners were injured or killed it was the Church members who ensured the family were fed and cared for. Thomas was known for his financial commitment to the Methodist Church of Campbell's Creek. Thomasina, like most women, was not named but was an active participant in caring and providing for those in need.

Thomas Boundy died at Campbells Creek in 1873. He is buried in 'Wesleyan Ground'. The first person buried in that particular section of this rather large cemetery. Several people with the family name of Boundy or Bishop are buried in close proximity in 'Wesleyan Ground'. Thomasina is a widow once more.

I'm not sure of the path Thomasina follows after Thomas' death. By about 1890 (and probably before) she is living in Maryborough. The Bishop and Hancock names are common in Maryborough and sometime during the late 1880s Lavinia and Richard are living there too.

Thomasina dies on January 15th 1898 aged ninety-six years of age. She is buried in the Maryborough cemetery. A Memorial Stone is erected on a large plot in the Methodist section.

Sacred to the Memory
Of
William Bishop
Who died Feb 9th 1878
Aged 51 years
Also
Eliza Jane Gill
Daughter of the above
Who died Sep 29th 1883
Aged 27 years
Also
Thamizine Boundy
Mother of the above William Bishop
Who died Jan 15th 1898
Aged 98 years
Also
Pte. Samuel R. Bishop
Son of the above
Killed in Gallipoli on Aug 10th 1915
Aged 44 years
His duty done
Also Thomas E. Bishop
Son of the above
Died Sep 24th 1937
Aged 68 years

*

The chasm between Thomasina and myself seems too wide for me to have any real understanding of her life. Yet, as I reflect on her baptism in the Gwennap Church on Christmas Day 1802 and her death in 1898, I suddenly realise Thomasina and I almost touch. For my paternal grandma was born in 1888. She would have visited her Great Grandma Thomasina in Maryborough as the family made regular trips from Avon Plains outside Donald. My grandma would have felt the warmth of Thomasina's touch, the warmth of her hug, just as I still remember the warmth of my grandma's touch and hug. We almost touch.

Like an excited child with a story 'on the tip of my tongue' I want to tell Thomasina I visited Thomas' grave in the Campbell's Creek Cemetery and I won't ever forget exactly where it is. It is right beside the marker of the 'Wesleyan Ground' and opposite the giant American Red Wood tree in the corner of the Church of England Ground. I know Thomasina won't have forgotten where her Thomas is buried but the giant tree was only sapling when her Thomas died and I want to tell her how very big it has grown since then. It is the biggest tree in the cemetery.

MY GREAT, GREAT, GREAT, GREAT GRANDMA

Dear Mum,

In Maryborough A Social History 1854–1904 the authors say 'In 1880 the average age of death in Victoria for males was thirty years and nine months and for females twenty-five years and four months.' How lucky are we having so many female forebears who lived such long lives. I know your mum died before she was forty, Phoebe was only 32 and Mary Ann left young children still needing a mother but what about those who lived into their seventies and eighties and those who were in the decade approaching triple figures.

When Martha and Richard and Sarah and Leonard migrated, their Australian born children never met their grandparents. Even in this we've been lucky. What about Thomasina and Thomas migrating in their late forties, their Australian grandchildren met them. Ann and John migrated in their sixties with one son already in Australia and many of their other children following. It was their English grandchildren who missed out on their company. But if children were missing out on developing grandparent relationships many of our female forebears had siblings or cousins who migrated. The extended family often maintained contact in their new land and often stayed in close geographical connections as well, which meant they could see each other regularly.

It was always fun looking through your calico bags of family photos. Who looked like their mum or dad or maybe a grandparent, the shape of a nose through the generations or men who went bald young and who was short and who was tall, how this person sang well but their sibling only mouthed the hymns in church, and how farming was a given as far back as we could trace.

We'd often talk about the strong Methodist link through the generations, of the forebear who actually heard John Wesley preach, the Cornish migrants who brought their Methodist beliefs with them, the Wiltshire migrants who clutched their Methodist ideals across the oceans, the Presbyterians and the Church of England travellers who carried their faith to their new land and the Catholics who maintained their link to their traditions. But we don't inherit faith, do we? Faith is a personal commitment yet when we hear the stories of women of faith their stories, their faith becomes imprinted, not in our DNA, but within us nevertheless. For their stories are part of our story so their faith story is part of our faith story, but we still have to make the personal commitment.

Faith communities were central to society and religion in many generations of our female forebears in a way they aren't today. Faith communities on the goldfields were there for families when miners were injured or killed, newcomers searched for their faith community, they knew it was one place they would belong, people like Harriet and William opened their home as a place of worship until a building was built. Lavinia's husband Richard donated land for a church, Ann's husband James, a carpenter and farmer helped build the church roof. Faith communities were not just for Sunday but every day of the week. Mary Ann and John were geographically isolated in a Shepherd's hut at Lake Wallace. It was an Anglican Chaplain from Portland who visited them baptising their three children including them in a faith community. We're lucky Mum, to be descended from these women of faith. From a very young age we acquired faith knowledge but more than that we acquired understanding of the significance and power of belonging to a community.

A love of rural living, dedication to family and lives committed to faith communities are threads linking us to our female forebears. Some were literate, others were not, some more likely to feel at home amongst the broken earth of the gold fields, others known to be more genteel, some quiet, some out-spoken, but I sense each was quite determined in their own way. What a rich heritage we have been gifted in the stories these women have passed through the generations.

Love, Judith

26
Ann Whiteway (Bickford)
1782 – 1876

Ann was in her early sixties when she arrived in Australia with her husband John, who was in his late sixties. John had been a tenant farmer in Modbury, Devon. They settled in South Australia where John died in 1851 in his mid-seventies. Ann died in 1876 in Northcote, a suburb of Melbourne, aged in her nineties.

I have to admit a slight bias here. When we were in England, I fell in love with the lush beauty of the Devon countryside and I could not understand why anyone would want to leave it. Modbury in itself is a beautiful village and the church which had been the faith home of the Bickfords and associated families was one that felt particularly welcoming. I spent time walking through the gravestones surrounding the church. A community gathering of the dead I felt an essence of my ancestors as they walked these paths to Church each Sunday and mourned those they loved amidst the gravestones, the tiny children they laid to rest and the elderly who had lived their lives within the faith and local community. I knew the name Modbury well from Dad's story of James Boon naming his farm Modbury. I had seen the name on the farm gate. Perhaps this was why I felt such an attachment to the village and the church, but as I pondered in the silence, I thought of my Gr. Gr. Gr. Gr. Grandma Ann and the last time she worshipped in this church, knowing she would never return. Did she take a final walk amidst the gravestones with John, paying their final respects to those who had lived in the place they were choosing to migrate from? My DNA may link me with Ann but amidst the moss eaten granite and lush grasses I felt a more personal connection.

Ann and John had nine children who lived to adulthood. One son had migrated before them. He was living in Victoria, but Ann and John chose to settle in South Australia. I suspect one of John's nephews was living there at the time and may have been standing on the dock to welcome as their ship arrived safely. Several of Ann and John's children joined them in Australia in the following years. Was that the plan? Were Ann and John to set up a home base for the family to join them? Were there reasons they chose not to migrate earlier? And why settle near a nephew when their son was in another state? None of us know what their long-term plan was.

One of Ann and John's sons, Rev James Bickford, was a Methodist Minister. He served as a missionary in the West Indies for fourteen years then migrated to Australia to be with family already here. One of their grandsons, a nephew to James, was a Methodist Minister too, Rev Edmund Sorrell Bickford, he migrated to Australia as young man. James and Edmund served the Methodist Church in many capacities during their lifetime. It would appear Ann and John were from families who looked beyond place that was familiar to the unknown.

In time I may discover some of the answers to my questions and maybe some will never be answered.

Ann is my final female forebear in my collection of women's stories. I wonder if it is the way it was meant to be, Ann and John making a journey those much younger did with trepidation. I gather and collate the stories of the women who live on in me, a task I have wanted to write for many years but now in my sixties I am fulfilling that yearning.

Am I meant to discover more of Ann or is her story in the journey she shared with her husband at a time in their life when many would expect them to lead a more sedate existence?

We live between two dates – our birth date and our death date. The number of years we have between those dates are an unknown figure, but we do know they are not infinite. Were Ann and John refusing to conform, refusing to be boxed and labelled and follow the expectations of the society in which they lived? Was it a yearning they'd always had to migrate or was it a feeling nudging at them in their later years?

When dementia was claiming Mum's mind, she was delighted to learn a second great grandchild was on the way. 'I'll have something to look forward to now,' she said. I wondered, is that what getting old is all about, having nothing to look forward to? Previously Mum always had something to look forward to, made plans for the next day or months ahead for a holiday or a special event, sometimes it was something as simple as making the time to read the latest book she had borrowed from the library or telephoning a friend for a chat. But as dementia addled her faculties she lost the capacity to make plans. Dementia had claimed her tomorrows.

Someone once said to me she had much on her 'bucket list' she wanted to achieve. Her ideal death would be to fulfil each and every item on her bucket list and to go to bed the night she crossed the last item off, go to sleep and not wake up in the morning. My 'bucket list' changes from time to time, items are added or deleted, some because I have fulfilled them others because they no longer seem important. There are those treasured moments not on my bucket list that leave an imprint within me I will forever cherish. I don't want to fulfil every item on my ever-changing bucket list. I don't want to ever reach a day in my life, a night in my life, when I have absolutely nothing else to look forward to.

Is that Ann and John's story? If not their story, is it the essence of their story? Did they want to see a place beyond their own back yard? Had the stories others told them about Australia tantalised their imaginations. Were there family or friends suggesting there were opportunities in this new land not available in the land of their birth? We live between two dates, from their decision to migrate in their sixties it appears Ann and John were not going to go sedately and calmly await the second date regretting what might have been. They not only had something to look forward to but actively pursued the fulfilment of that event. Age was no barrier to their plans.

Ann died in April 1876. Her death announcement reads:

'BICKFORD – on the 12th inst., at her son's, Mr. N. M. Bickford's residence, Edmeston-villa, Northcote, Ann Whitemay, relict of the late Mr. John Bickford, formerly of Edmeston, Barton, Modbury, Devon, England, in her 96th year.'

Her grandson, James, by then a farmer at Avon Plains, outside Donald, had named his property Modbury. The son who was caring for Ann in her final years named his home Edmeston-villa. Their names, their stories, linking their beginnings and their new place half-way around the world.

I'd like to know more of Ann's story, the sixty plus years she lived before migrating and the almost thirty years in her chosen land. The gap between her living and mine is not only the number of years but the life experiences of different eras. Yet, negotiating the retirement years as they are often now called, can be tricky, when work no longer dictates the routine of the days and weeks, when those newly retired have to plan or discover what they will look forward to tomorrow, next week or in the years to come. I have no plans or desire to migrate but whenever I think of Ann I am reminded being older does not mean being confined and sedate. The end date is not known but we do have control over the life we live before it comes.

I salute you, Gr. Gr. Gr. Gr. Grandma Ann.

27
Neatening the Threads

'To forget one's ancestors is to be a brook without a source, a tree without a root.'
— **Chinese proverb**

Dear Mum,

'Inherited Touch' is complete. The stories of your mum and grandma have been told, amongst those of all my female forebears who chose to migrate to Australia or were born here. My promise to you is fulfilled. I'm not sure you would be totally comfortable with all I have revealed. You kept much to yourself about the first ten years of your life, until your final years, when dementia peeled away the layers. I wish dementia had not claimed you, but none of us had any control over that. Yet as I struggled to find you amidst the dementia-created anger and vindictiveness, you gave me the most precious gift of a glimpse into those early years and the women who nurtured you to be the person you were.

Resilience is the ability to bungy jump through life. You and I are the least likely candidates to join a bungy jumping queue! But life itself has presented each of us, each of the women in this book with experiences sending us hurtling over the edge, plummeting earthward at a fear-inducing speed to be yanked upwards by the elastic bungy ropes only to plummet earthward once again. It was only in the vulnerabilities of the women I recognised their resilience. It was only in accepting my own vulnerabilities I recognise my resilience. It was only when you gifted me the glimpse of the first ten years of your life I fully understood the depth of your sadness in the loss of your mum. Resilience is not the ability to get up when the sun is shining each morning, it is getting up day after day when the skies are a thunderous black, believing one morning, eventually, a tiny ray of sunlight will finally pierce the dark.

In gathering these stories, I've felt a wonderfully delicious sense of belonging to a community of imperfect and ordinary women. What a blessing the words imperfect and ordinary are! Yet, the blessing is beyond their imperfections and ordinariness. As my duster flicks the mundane and history's perception of women from the words it reveals our female forebears with significant stories to tell beyond the years of their living. Some remembered as strong and feisty, others formidable or damaged, their stories, their personalities are not forgotten. They struggled and thrived, knew pain and sorrow, joy and laughter. Can you imagine all these women in one room at the same time? What stories would be added to what we already know as these women talk and talk and talk and talk. 'Inherited Touch' may be complete but there are countless stories yet to be added to the lives of these women who lived before us and will live on in those who come after us.

I'm neatening the threads, but they aren't tied as though the fabric is complete. The stories continue with the generations, their lives still in their early years, the generations yet to be born.

You will probably laugh at this Mum but I'm coming to realise I'm now in the older generation. As your and Dad's generation of the family die it is my generation filling that 'older' role. Is this when wisdom supposedly invades my being? When I visited you at Yarriambiack Lodge I would always say, 'Hello Mum,' as I entered your room. 'Hello Judith,' you would respond. Then you would stare at me as if you weren't sure who I was. 'Do I look older than you think I should?' I unwisely asked you once. 'Yes, you are,' was your emphatic but honest reply. I did laugh as I said, 'you don't have to be too honest about it.' But dementia had claimed you too much by then for you to get the joke. You always remembered my voice though.

Now you are gone beyond my touch, beyond reading the letters I've written for this book. But the stories are not gone. They keep the women of the stories beside me, keep you beside me, as you shared my desire to record the stories of my female forebears. 'How's the book going?' you'd ask me every time I saw you. I always had some excuse or reason why it wasn't finished. Sometimes an idea needs time to percolate, to mature, like the Christmas cake needs time to mature to attain its rich flavour. Was I waiting for a little of that wisdom which supposedly comes with age to invade my being before I could the stories justice? Or perhaps it is like the gentle hope of Ecclesiastes (3: 1-8) 'for everything there is a season'.

For 'Inherited Touch' the season has come. It is complete.

Love,

Judith

PS. I almost forgot to tell you how well Dad's orchids are doing now. Remember how he sent them back to my place during the drought as your town water was causing them to shrivel and die. I re-potted, watered and fertilised them. In all those years I only got one very small, single flower spike on one pot. But this year two pots had a single flower spike and the third pot had two. Each of them so heavy with the number of flowers they carried I had to put stakes in the pots to support the flower spikes. I'd forgotten when the earth is ravaged by drought, flood or fire it takes time for the earth to heal to nourish the plants again. Just as it took time for the orchids to heal before they could bloom in all their splendour again.

Orchids belonging to Judith's Dad, Stan Avery.

RESOURCES

Deveson, Ann *Resilience*, Allen & Unwin, 2003

Enright, Anne *The Long Gaze Back* edited by Sinead Gleeson, New Island, 2015

Jenkin, Constance & McGennis, Ann *A Parent's Treasure Chest – Exploring the Path to Resilicence*, Commonwealth Department of Health and Aged Care, 2000

Osborn, Betty & DuBourg, Trenear *Maryborough*, Central Goldfields Shire Council, 2011

Nostalgia Reedy Creek compiled by Reedy Creek Progress Association, published 1982

Patterson, Adrian, *Visage Artistic Applications* (representation of Mary Murphy from convict records)

ACKNOWLEDGEMENTS

For that most precious gift – a sense of belonging to a group of women who understand the journey – I thank the members of Carpe Diem and Spring (SWWV) for sharing my writing path. My scrap booking friends I have known for longer than I care to admit, for sharing life's broader path and to the Luminaries who share my breast cancer walk.

To the local historians and historical societies in Cavendish, Hamilton, Warracknabeal, St Arnaud, Donald, Birchip, Ararat, Maryborough, Talbot, Clunes and Castlemaine, I thank you for your vast knowledge and willingness to share that knowledge. To the caretaker at Campbell's Creek Cemetery who spent a bitterly cold morning locating the graves I was looking for and telling me about the giant Redwood tree, I give my special thanks.

To my fellow family historians and interest groups at Family History Connections in Blackburn who understand the importance of connecting with those who have gone before us, I acknowledge your guidance.

27. ACKNOWLEDGEMENTS

To friends I've known a long time and those new to my female circle I cherish our friendships and your belief this book was worth writing.

To extended family members, Auntie Laurel, Faye and Jim, your care, warmth and kindness at a difficult time is not forgotten and will always remain a part of my story.

To Mum and Dad, no longer here to read this, your stories remind me of where I have come from.

To Michael, the love of my life, who has listened to my grumblings when the words wouldn't come but was wise enough to offer little comment, who tolerated the many hours I've spent at the computer, I give you my endless thanks.

To our sons and their wives, Peter and Aimee, David and Julie, your stories are the next generation of stories connecting the ever-expanding family circle.

To our grandson Rohan, who often asks, 'How's the writing going Ma?' and our granddaughter Tessa who extends the female line, these stories are to remind you of where you have come from as you look forward to all the tomorrows you have yet to experience.

To Jasmine and Shani, your DNA connects you to other families but families are not limited to only those connected by DNA. You are part of our family story, blended into our family relationships and always welcome.

To Blaise and the team at Busybird, I thank you not just for the excellent job of publishing my book but more importantly I thank you for sharing my journey.

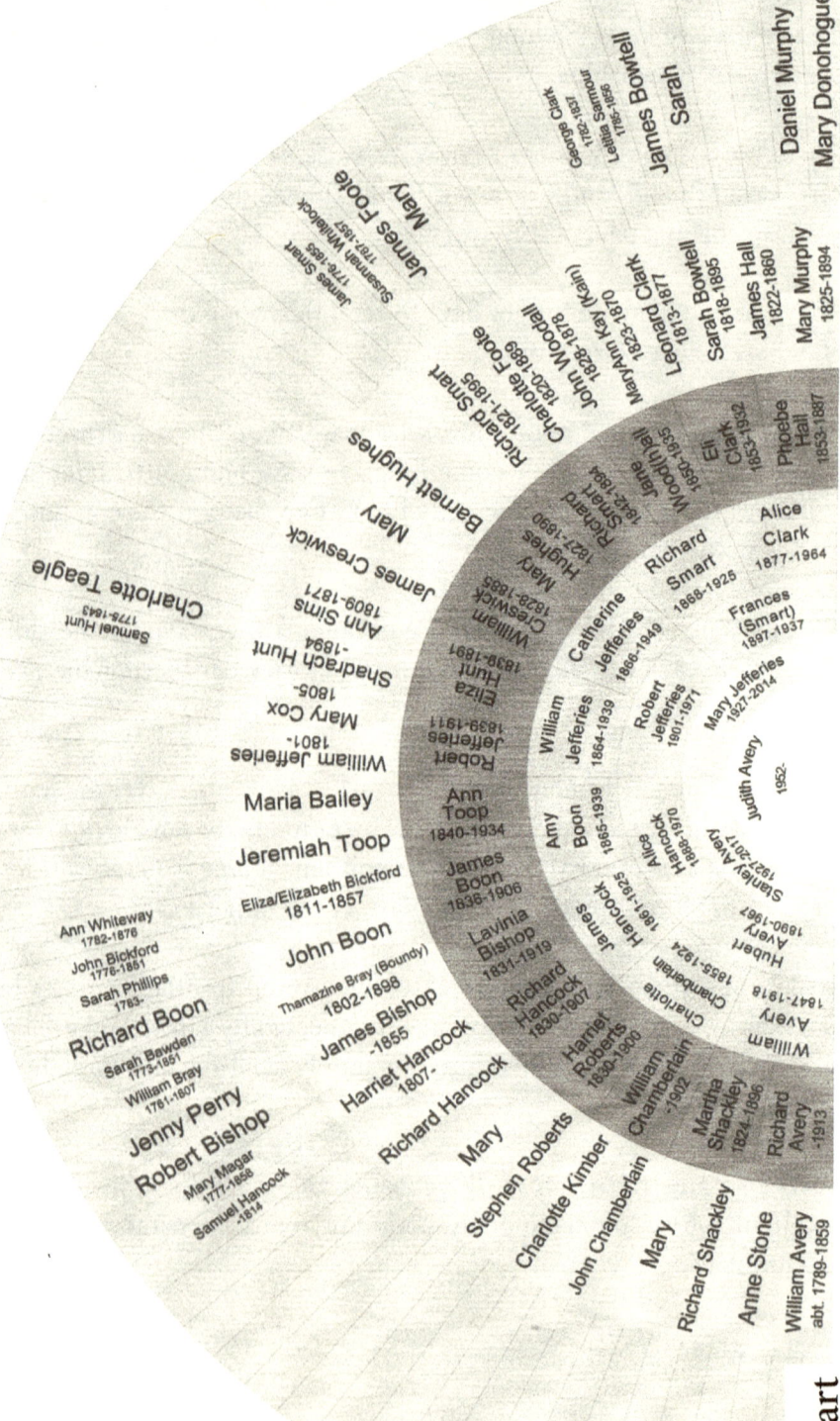

Family Chart

www.ingramcontent.com/pod-product-compliance
Lightning Source LLC
Chambersburg PA
CBHW021437080526
44588CB00009B/558